To Denise,

In memory of my grandfather,

Jean Bailey Gaede

St. Paul's
across Thames.
1928

Henry T. Bailey

YANKEE CONVICTIONS

THE LIFE AND TIMES OF HENRY TURNER BAILEY "THE CHEERFUL DEAN"

Compiled and edited by Jean Bailey Gaede

Special appreciation to Michael Uyesugi for his time and graphic expertise in completing the successful production and printing of this book. Additional thanks for editing to Linda Tuthill, Gretchen Gaede, and Mary Bailey.

Yankee Convictions: The Life and Times of Henry Turner Bailey, "The Cheerful Dean" / Jean Bailey Gaede

ISBN 978-1-4675-9008-2

Manufactured in the United States of America
First Edition 2013

1 3 5 7 9 10 8 6 4 2

CONTENTS

Note: Henry Turner Bailey frequently signed drawings and letters with his initials. Often HTB has been used to identify him throughout the book.

Ravenna
1924

Henry T Bailey

PREFACE

MY FATHER AND MOTHER often told my brothers and me stories about our Grandfather, Henry Turner Bailey, illustrating his personality and character. We learned from his writings of his humor, his reverence for nature and his love of the beautiful. Although he died when I was barely four years old, I have always felt as though I had known him.

This portrait has been reinforced by several visits to North Scituate, Massachusetts and to HTB's home, "Trustworth," where his personality seemed to be still in residence even seventy years after his death.

When the *New York Times* reviewed his book, *Yankee Notions*, they said that it should be called "Yankee Convictions" so strong were his values and his beliefs.

For this reason and because his life reflected his philosophy, I have named this biography, *Yankee Convictions: The Life and Times of Henry Turner Bailey, "The Cheerful Dean."*

This book is dedicated to the memory of his and Josephine's five children, now all deceased: Elisabeth, Lawrence, Theodore, Margaret and Gilbert. What a superb childhood they had in the fields of North Scituate along the shores of the Atlantic, guided by devoted, creative and hard working parents. They led enviable lives in an atmosphere of freedom that belongs to a bygone era.

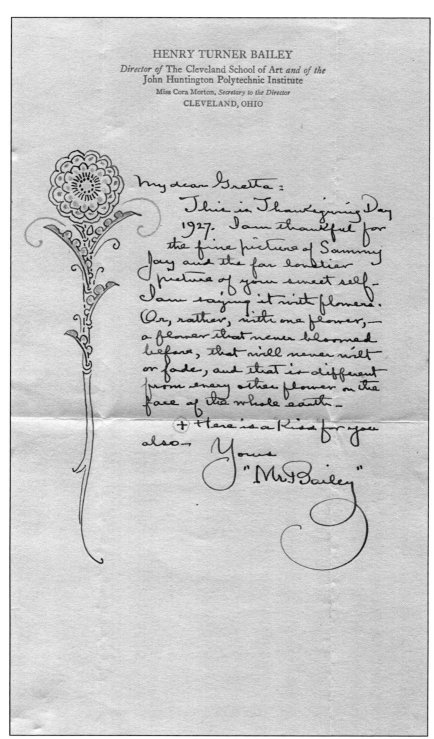

My dear Gretta:

This is Thanksgiving Day 1927. I am thankful for the fine picture of Sammy Jay and the far lovelier picture of your sweet self—I am saying it with flowers. Or, rather, with one flower,—a flower that never bloomed before, that will never wilt or fade, and that is different from every other flower on the face of the whole earth—

+ Here is a Kiss for you also—

Yours

"Mr. Bailey"

Letter to Gretta from HTB with his characteristic handwriting and adornment.

INTRODUCTION

THIS BIOGRAPHY OF MY GRANDFATHER, Henry Turner Bailey, is in part a compilation of the writings of others in the family who have attempted to capture the essence of this strong and creative man. All I have heard and read about him convinces me that what he provided for his family and all those around him was a strong moral compass for life.

In addition to HTB's own powerful writing, I have been the beneficiary of the writing skills of family members going back to his grandmother, Sarah, his own mother, Eudora, his sister, Sally, his daughter, Margaret and his grandson, Paul, all of whose writings I have quoted extensively because they bring a freshness and originality that could not be duplicated.

I am also indebted to HTB's secretary, Ruth Johnson, who gave me her collection of HTB books and letters; and to my father, Ted Bailey, who compiled a scrapbook of clippings from newspapers from around the country of stories about his father and his many lectures; and to Raymond Kelley, a dear Cleveland friend whose daughter, Kay Sullivan, gave me Mr. Kelley's collection of letters from Henry and Josephine as well as photographs, paintings and a bust of my grandfather; and to Gretta Pallister whose father, C. M. Shipman, was a close friend in the Burroughs Club of Willoughby. Gretta gave me photographs and illustrated letters she received as a little girl from HTB.

At a house sale in Cleveland, an artist friend discovered a whole file of original Christmas cards that Henry and Josephine had sent, and the owner, upon learning of my existence, gave them to the artist to give to me.

My brother, Jack Bailey, some years ago, tracked down a portrait of HTB that he heard was owned by the Huntington Foundation. He found it on the floor behind a water cooler somewhat damaged. When he offered to buy it, he was told he could have it, so he had it restored and reframed. The large oil portrait by Cleveland artist, Rolf Stoll, is considered one of his best.

Additional information has come from fellow Chautauquan, Av Posner, the Cleveland Museum of Art, the Cleveland Institute of Art, the Chautauqua Archives, the University of Oregon and the Scituate Historical Society.

ABOUT THE WRITER

JEAN BAILEY GAEDE is a granddaughter of Henry Turner Bailey and Josephine Litchfield Bailey, and daughter of Theodore (Ted) Bailey and Helen Moyle Bailey. Upon her parents' marriage in 1920, they settled in Cleveland, where Henry Turner Bailey was Director of the Cleveland School of Art (now the Cleveland Institute of Art).

The two families lived side-by-side on East 84th street until 1930 when HTB retired from the Cleveland School of Art and Henry and Josephine, Beth and Gilbert returned to Trustworth. Ted and Helen and their three children, Jim, Jack and Jean moved to the Cleveland suburb of Shaker Heights.

Jean and her late husband, Bob (Robert C. Gaede)—an architect well known in the field of Historic Preservation—have two children, Gretchen and Carl. Jean has been active in civic affairs, serving as a member of the Shaker Heights Board of Education, President of the Metropolitan YWCA of Cleveland and President of the Women's City Club of Cleveland. She now resides at Park Lane Villa, a restored historic building in University Circle, the cultural hub of Cleveland. Summers are spent at Chautauqua, New York where Henry Turner Bailey was Director of the School of Art from 1906 to 1916. Members of the fifth generation of the family still enjoy Chautauqua and the 100 year old cottage her parents bought in 1947.

Jean is the author of *Ancestral Anthology*, a compilation of writing by seven generations of female lineal descendants of her great-great-grandmother, Sarah Tilden Turner, including a total of fifteen writers of prose and poetry spanning the years from 1810 to 2004.

PUTTING THE PIECES TOGETHER - A PERSONAL REFLECTION

THE ONLY MEMORY I HAVE of my grandfather is of sitting on his lap when I was barely four years old and watching him cut out a string of paper dolls for me. He took his small scissors from his pocket and quickly, as if by magic, produced them. Though this is but one memory, I feel as though I know him. I have heard so many stories about him. Reinforcing this feeling are all the memorabilia and letters that friends and family have given me. When he was Director of the Cleveland School of Art, a sculptor from Russia by the name of Alexander Blazy did a bust of Dean Bailey, as he was known, and years later I was given a plaster cast of the bust. It resides in my living room where occasionally my daughter will surprise me by placing a hat or scarf on his head. The original is at the Cleveland Institute of Art. I learned this when taking courses there after graduating from high school. I didn't want anyone to know my connection with Grandpa because I felt too much would be expected of me. Paul Travis was my teacher for life drawing. One day I was just sitting there and he came up behind me and said, "Why aren't you drawing?" I replied, "I'm just not in a creative mood." Then he said, "What would your grandfather say?" "How do you know who my grandfather was?" Mr. Travis replied, "There's a bust of him in the men's room and you look just like him!" (Hopefully this bronze bust now resides in the a more appropriate place in a much expanded building.)

Perhaps the most important artifact that I have is the Rolf Stoll oil portrait of my grandfather that my brother had restored.

In it, Grandpa sits erect in a three piece suit, chain hanging down from vest pocket, stick pin in his tie, thin steel-rimmed glasses held in his right hand, his eyes twinkling and a slight smile upon his lips. It is almost life size and we tried putting him in the dining room, but his presence was so strong that it was like having another person at the dinner table prompting us to find a more appropriate place in the front hall.

Every morning, when the portrait still hung in our Shaker Heights home, I would place my hands behind my back as my grandfather and my father were wont to do and say good morning to Grandpa. His eyes seemed to follow me wherever I went. Sometimes he seemed pleased with me and other times he seemed to be saying, "What are you doing of value today?" echoing one of his beliefs that a person's true character is shown by what he does with his leisure time.

Whether at his home, Trustworth in Massachusetts, or any other place that he graced, his presence is still felt. His sense of humor, his philosophy, his love of nature and of the beauty of the world, and his writings about family still enrich all who knew him. Hopefully my biography of this renaissance man will serve to continue his legacy and inspiring influence. Putting the pieces together to accurately reflect his character has not been easy but the joy of discovery has rewarded me many times over.

Eudora, Henry Turner Bailey's mother.

CHAPTER I
CHILDHOOD

When I close my eyes I can see a group of people about an open fire in the house where I was born. It is Sunday evening at twilight. There is my father with his ebony flute with silver keys, my mother with a baby in her arms, my dear old Aunt Sarah with little Albert by her side, and there sits Fred and here am I. We are singing softly:

> Soon we'll gather by the river;
> Soon our pilgrimage will cease;
> Soon our happy hearts will quiver
> With the melody of peace.
> —HTB from *The Magic Realm of the Arts*

Henry Turner Bailey—gifted artist, teacher, writer and engaging lecturer—was born on December 9, 1865 in the little shore town of Scituate, Massachusetts just south of Boston. He came into the world in the home of his paternal grandmother, Hannah Wade Bailey, who had lost her husband and four of her children by the time she was thirty-eight. His maternal grandmother, Sarah Tilden married William Turner when she was twenty. In her youth she wrote a poem responding to the hard life of the times:

MUSIC
Blest Melody, how oft thy powerful strains
Have raised my sad desponding heart, when grief
Had weighed it down
Almost to hate of being. Oh how oft
When all was dull and tasteless—when my book
Was thrown aside, and not a single friend
Of converse rational, was nigh to chase
With cheering talk—the tedious hours away;
How oft, Oh Music! has thy heavenly voice
Dispelled each black idea, and suppressed
Each restless passion.

SARAH TILDEN TURNER DIED in 1845 at the age of thirty-five. Her death left five children motherless. Among them was Eudora Turner who was to marry Charles Edward Bailey, son of Hannah Wade Bailey. Together Eudora and Charles had seven children. Henry was the oldest of four boys and three girls.

Henry's brothers and sisters were: Frederick, Albert, Charles, Sarah, and Emma. A seventh child, Bertha, died at four years of age. They were all raised with love, religion, respect for nature and dedication to work.

From a biography of HTB by Margaret Bailey Miles:
Shortly before Henry's birth, scarlet fever had caused the death, on the same day, of Eudora's two brothers; Charles Turner the sixth—age nine, and Henry Turner—age fourteen, the latter adored by his big sister. So when Eudora's baby proved to be a boy, she named him Henry Turner Bailey."

Henry writes in *Yankee Notions:*
She (his mother Eudora) fell in love with a black-haired young man who called at the house for eggs. He had fallen in love with her at sight. They married in six months and went to live in his mother's house where, a full year later, I, their first son was born.

Of course my first and best friends were my parents. Life seemed to me so full of delight, so fascinating, such a great game to play, that I shall never cease to be grateful that they brought me into this world—with the help of old Doctor Thomas who charged them $50 C.O.D..

From *Yankee Notions,* Henry describes his mother:
My childhood was dominated by my adorable mother. She had long golden brown hair as glossy as feathers. Her cheeks were rosy. Her large gray eyes had sparkles in them. She was always busy. With four baby boys under ten years old; with that fearsome old lady, Grandma Bailey, sitting up in bed, her black cap above a pair of critical eyes that snapped upon me through silver rimmed spectacles to be good to every day; with that black bearded man in blue overalls and jumper and great grain-leather Russian boots to above his knees striding in from the mill three times a day to be fed and kissed; with all the washing and mending and making over clothes for me and my brothers, she just had to be busy. But she managed to find time to sit in the twilight, with two babies in her lap and two others by her side, and recite poetry to us. How we loved Hiawatha.

Henry describes his father:
A jolly man in blue jeans and big Russian military boots who approved of me. He used to catch me up to ride upon his shoulder. He used to say things to my mother, the Woman-who-loved-poetry, that made her eyes twinkle and her cheeks blush. Then he would kiss her.

Mother always regarded me with amused consternation. She never knew what I might do next. With something of her love of the poetic plus a little of my father's trick of getting things done, I appeared to be too imaginative and reckless.

Christmas Day, 1884 as described by Henry's sister, Sarah (Sally) Bailey Brown:
(Because it would be difficult, if not impossible to duplicate the vivid picture she draws in more contemporary words, her recollections are quoted in their entirety.)

Christmas 1884. Two big boys in the parlor, sick with measles and whooping cough. Not much room for the four-poster bed brought down from the spare room for the occasion, with the air-tight stove and Father's desk and the big Town safe, for Father was Town Clerk and kept all the things in the parlor. Two younger boys sick in the little bedroom. Allie (Albert) had it bad. He had grown eight inches in the last year and Charlie called him a bean-pole. They were afraid he would go into decline and already Scotts Emulsion of Cod Liver Oil had been prescribed. It was fun to see Mother get it down him.

Two little girls in the spool bed in the corner of the sitting-room and over by the bay window a sick little baby in her crib, a baby that wasn't going to get well. Father, Mother and Little Auntie, someone always there in the high-backed rocker to give drinks of water in the long nights. Neighbors were kind and Freddie's girl sent a wonderful basket of fruit, big oranges, red bananas and dates. He and Henny (Henry) were getting better and spent hours playing checkers with a board and men that they had made themselves. They could make anything.

The stockings weren't very full that Christmas morning. Sarah woke early. The light was shining across the roof of the store down the street and someone was rattling the stove in the kitchen. There was a strange looking object over in the corner. It looked like a cart on wheels. There was a little walnut cradle too, with sister's rag doll, Patsy, in it and a bedstead with Sarah's own Dinah in it. They had had their faces painted. Mother said she was afraid they would get the measles and all the time they were having their faces painted. They looked beautiful. Henny who was going to be an artist, had painted them with his real paints and now you could scrub their faces and the paint wouldn't come off. Some rich relatives had handed down the cart and cradle but big brother had made the bed. Just like the four poster in the bedroom, the posts turned on Father's lathe and strings across to hold the feather mattress Mother had made. Real sheets and a piece of home-spun blanket and a coverlet cut out at the corners, like Mother's. It just fit Dinah.

Christmas was mostly like Sunday so Father had family prayers after breakfast. He sat near the three doors so every one could hear. "And there were in that same country, shepherds abiding in the fields, keeping watch over their flocks by night." It was nice, lying in bed and listening. The prayer was long for Father was a Deacon and there was lots to speak to the Lord about.

The singing wasn't as good as usual for Allie was too sick to play the organ and everyone's throat was sore and Mother couldn't carry a tune, but Father's voice was beautiful, like hollering down a rain barrel as he sang, *Joy to the World*. There was a big piece of the dear family pig roasted for dinner and applesauce and the vegetables that the boys had hoed all summer, and so many pies! The pie closet up in the back chamber was full of them. Cranberry was the handsomest with the red showing between the strips of crust, V-shaped like the boys' suspenders where they buttoned on.

It was dark early. Henny was going out for the first time. He was going to take Josie to the sociable at Church. She had yellow hair and played the organ. It was dark now and quiet, only the light from the hanging lamp in the kitchen shone into the sitting-room and the boys had all stopped fighting. The funny glass in the front of the stove made pretty pictures of red and blue and green light. It was a nice Christmas, if only little sister wouldn't whoop so, it scared you when she got black in the face, but everybody was better, except for the baby.

Henry's sister, Sarah, also wrote the following about her brother:
Henry's roots went deep into the soil of old New England. His family tree received life from Governor William Bradford, Humphrey Turner, Peregrine White, Elder Brewster, Nathaniel Tilden and Robert Stetson, the Cornet of the Plymouth Colony Troopers, who fought against the Indians. Henry was always a brilliant and active child. His mother said often, "Henry if you will sit still five minutes, I will give you five cents." He never earned the five cents.

His father was a visionary, always inventing new gadgets, starting new business ventures and never had any money. He was sharply criticized by his more practical neighbors for buying books and machinery for his boys, for he always directed and encouraged all the activities of his children. They designed wall brackets and sawed them out with their jig-saw and made many things turning them out on the lathe. When Henry was fourteen and Frederic twelve they had a flourishing job printing business. Albert, the third boy, was really good on the old organ. Fred played the violin and Charles the bass viol. Henry, they decided, might play the triangle and he came in on the off beat with enthusiasm. It was something to hear them play *Marching Through Georgia*.

One of the joys in the life of the little sisters was to ride on Big Brother's feet. They sat astride his foot and with their arms clasped around his leg they were raced from one room to another.

To his mother he was always the duckling that turned out to be a swan, and yet she delighted to puncture any sign of an inflated ego in her son. On one of his last weekend visits to her as she lay in her little white bed, a little white-haired old lady of ninety, he said, "I don't know whether to go to church this morning or stay with you." She said, 'You had better to go church. I've had about all I can stand this morning."

Henry writes in *Yankee Notions*:
Living in the old home whence all but she had fled, the woman-who-loved-poetry now in her ninetieth year, still finds life exciting.

Eudora at age 90.

Eudora wrote the following poem (after a period of illness when she was seldom seen outside the house):

> I'm tired of being patient
> And trying to be good;
> I am tired of toast and gruel
> and all such mushy food.
>
> I am tired of pills and tonics,
> Of resting and "Oh dears,"
> I am tired of being nothing
> All these long weary years
>
> I want to be a girl again
> And run barefoot and wild
> And paddle in that little brook
> As when I was a child;
>
> To lay my cheek against the ground
> Under the giant pines
> And catch the perfume of the woods,
> Hemlocks and wild grapevines
>
> To see those curious Indian pipes,
> And watch the glint and shine
> On waters of the dear old pond
> Through the branches of the pine.
>
> "Sweet fields beyond the swelling flood"
> Could never fairer be;
> Nor golden streets or gates of pearl
> Seem lovelier to me.
>
> Before I lay this mortal by
> I would like, if I could,
> Once more to rest my tired head
> Up there in father's wood.

Eudora lived to the age of ninety-one, dying in 1930.

Henry and Josephine when they were young and engaged.

CHAPTER II
GROWING UP AND MARRIAGE

"From the age of four, Henry loved a little playmate, Josephine Litchfield." —Margaret Bailey Miles

HENRY'S DAUGHTER, MARGARET, WROTE a biography of her father for the Scituate Historical Society. She tells about his life when his father, Charles Bailey, sold the general store that Hannah Wade Bailey had run until her death, and he moved the mill and the family to 754 Country Way and made the mill over into a home for his family. Although the father was glad to relinquish the general store, "the income from his various optimistic schemes for self-employment was often meager. He had some success, however, in his shop next door where he sold watches, clocks, jewelry and sewing machines."

Henry writes in *Yankee Notions:*
Then there was Josephine. My first memory of her is of a slim little golden-haired creature in whose back yard, beneath a blossoming apple tree, I used to make mud pies and play keep house. That must have been in May after we were four years old... . We were pals from the first. I was father to all her dolls before we ever went to school.

IN SCHOOL HENRY EXCELLED in reading and writing, but Josephine surpassed him in arithmetic and spelling. Margaret writes of his preoccupation with drawing pictures behind his geography book.

Upon graduation from High School, at age sixteen, Henry and Josephine became engaged. (They both graduated at the top of their class.) Josephine played the organ at the Baptist Church and taught grade school in the Egypt section of Scituate. When Henry gave his graduation speech, he realized that the audience was silent and listening to his every word and for the first time he felt, as he writes in his essay *Victorious Surrender*, "the delicious sting of power, power over the minds of his fellow men. Is that the power to make vegetables grow? No that is the power to make men grow."

He entered the Massachusetts Normal Art School in 1883 and graduated in 1887, earning his way by teaching in Boston night schools and supervising art in the public schools of Lowell. He was only 22 when he was appointed the first State Supervisor of Drawing in Massachusetts—a position in which he delighted for sixteen years.

Henry and Josephine were engaged for a period of seven years while they both worked to establish themselves.

From Margaret Bailey Miles' biography of HTB:
In their spare time they went botanizing together. One may smile at this, but eighty years later piles of folders containing pressed specimens, each neatly labeled with its Latin name, attest to the fact that the lovers kept their minds, to some extent, on their botanizing. They were dreaming too, for Henry designed an unusual and rather ambitious house and persuaded a reluctant land-owner to sell him a few acres of blueberry pasture on Booth Hill on which to build it.

In *Yankee Notions*, Henry writes:
When I told her (his mother, Eudora) that I had decided to build a home in Aunt Lydia's Huckleberry pasture on Booth Hill, Mother said, "Well, you might as well have staked out a house on the moon. She will never sell it to you." Then after a moment she added, "But perhaps you will get it. The Lord has some spoiled children."

Henry writes about this period of Josephine's and his courtship:
Under a syringa bush in Groveland Cemetery one Sunday noon we agreed to work for a real home. Lovely June held the South Shore in its arms. The air was sweet with the breath of the sea and of the blossoming grape vines, the sweet briar roses, and the syringa. The little golden-haired girl, with whom I had played since childhood now grown to be organist in the church sat on soft grass at my side, and very close to me. We exchanged syringa blossoms! I still have her spray pressed between the leaves of my Bible and on the eighteenth of June every year since forty-seven years now, she has worn in her hair a fresh spray that I have given her.

Margaret Bailey Miles writes:
Josephine and Henry pooled their savings and hired Henry's uncle, Waldo Turner, to build the house "according to the rather unusual specifications. They moved in the night they were married in September 1889, naming it Trustworth, because they felt it was worth trusting God for all those seven years.

THE HOUSE STILL STANDS today where it was built. It is shingle-style and reflective of the Arts and Crafts movement. The design is inventive with a forerunner of the picture window, but in this case taking the shape of a semi-circle. Another window, circular in shape, abides next to the front staircase where it appears to be rolling down the wainscoting. A stained glass window decorates the dining room. In the living room, the fireplace is brick and the opening is shaped like a key-hole with "Trustworth" carved on the wood mantel above. A studio for painting (once a nursery) is situated over the porte-cochere with a small staircase winding down to Henry's study—located on the other side of the driveway. Here is Henry's huge, unique desk with cubbyholes and shelves to organize the product of his creative and restless mind.

A great granddaughter of Henry Turner Bailey and daughter of Josephine and Howard Schuman, Elisabeth Tova Bailey wrote the following poem when she was in high school:

TRUSTWORTH
All the rooms are musty and old.
Sunlight streams in the windows
to shine on the bare wooden floor,
baking the boards just as it has
for a hundred years.

The sun doesn't reach the dark corners
of the room or the hidden cubby
holes and drawers in my
great-grandfather's studio.

Every year we return
rediscovering the same things,
old pens and bottles of ink and ancient paper
and funny things that aren't made any more.

There is a desk with dozens of little drawers
and among the ancient newsprint on a secret
low-to-the-floor shelf there is always a soft
round nest with a new generation of mice.

I look through the many carefully pressed
flowers great-grandfather collected,
memories of fields in bright sun,
a century ago.

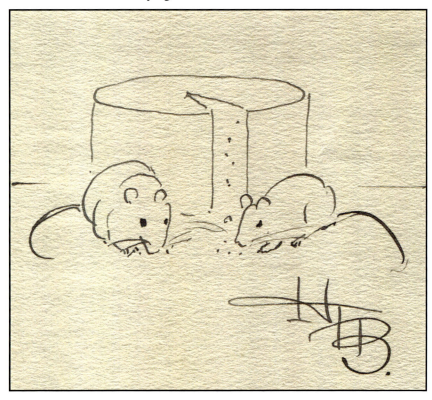

EQUALLY INTERESTING AS HTB'S STUDY is the attic of the house
which is topped by a tower accessible by a ladder-like stair and a trap door.
The tower has windows all around and when the house was built, one could
see the ocean and the ships at sea. As a child visiting, I was awed by this
tower and in my memory, it was atop at least two or three attics, it seemed
so high up to me. When I returned as an adult, I was surprised to see that it
was much more constrained than I had remembered. Now the open fields are
filled with trees, obscuring the view of the ocean. But somehow the magic
of the tower remains and I found it just as fascinating as when I was a child.

Home designed by HTB for his bride, Josephine, completed in 1889, the day of their wedding. North Scituate, Massachusetts.

Elisabeth (in front), with Lawrence, Margaret and Theodore (in back). Photo taken before Gilbert was born.

CHAPTER III
HENRY AND JOSEPHINE'S CHILDREN

"Children need to see beauty in the open, alive, under the inspirational leadership of a lover of life. A stuffed bird or a pressed flower, is as inadequate for developing a love of these things as is a moth on a pin."
—HTB in *Yankee Notions*

In *Yankee Notions*, Henry writes:
Mrs. Bailey and I have five children—three boys and two girls—Elisabeth, Lawrence, Theodore, Margaret and Gilbert. They all have a love of beauty and are attempting to make beautiful the work of their hands.

When the children were small they were our constant companions outdoors. In the home library are fascinating illustrated pamphlets, handmade, giving detailed accounts of days spent and the Musquashcut river in the big family canoe of Cohasset Harbor. These pamphlets contain lists of the birds we saw and of the trees and flowers we identified. For thirty years before coming to Cleveland, I persistently refused flattering offers of positions in large cities at double the salary I was receiving because Mrs. Bailey and I believed our children should have the advantage of a home in the country, where experiences with nature at first hand would permanently enrich their lives. This enrichment took place without their knowledge. They received a sort of surreptitious education. Every spring in early April we used to cut a sod from the east pasture, a circular sod, six inches in diameter, and fit it into a Japanese bowl we had, with little kittens on the rim looking inward. This we placed on the table in the dining room and kept it watered. Out of it would grow a sedge, a grass or two, a violet, a cudweed, a cinquefoil, a wild strawberry, an aster or a goldenrod, and three or four other plants—each spring a new surprise for us. We used to bring in single plants pot them and watch them develop. It was more fascinating than a movie to put one of these on a sunny window ledge, draw a white shade in front of it, and study its shadow cast on the curtain.

Portrait of Baby Beth.

HTB gives readers a glimpse of his love for his children and the careful nurturing of their development into compassionate and thoughtful human beings in his book, *When Little Souls Awake.*

One chapter has to do with his eldest child, Beth, although he disguises her identity by calling her Dorothy. The chapter is called "My First Bereavement." HTB, at this time, was away much of the time so that his days at home took on even more meaning.

He writes:
How delicious it was, after days of absence, to hold her (Beth) soft, warm, sweet little bunch of a body in my arms again and rock her to sleep! By the time she was two years old I had learned to expect, when I entered the house, a sudden rush from the stairway, a sudden raid from the hall. I was always called upon to sit and deliver a story. I can see her now in the chimney corner, her little brother on her arm, listening with wide eyes and bated breath to the legends of Greek heroes and Norse kings, until the twilight was lost in night and the firelight danced our shadows on the walls. Later she used to call me to her room for the good-night kiss. She would whisper to me, "Won't you read to me tonight? Just one more chapter, please?"

Thus for seven rosy years — and they seemed to me but a few days, for the love I had for her — we sailed together on our journeys.

This evening when she was eight years old, I came home from a long journey, hungry for the sight of her. There was no rush of her flying feet to meet me at the gate. Where is she I asked? She had gone to her chamber. I would go up at once to bid her goodnight. I took a volume as I passed on to her door. I knocked gently. No response. I knocked again. Not a sound from within. Opening the door softly I looked toward her bed. Oh, my poor heart! What a revelation!

There was her body, propped amid the pillows, her loved face, graced with drapery of flowing hair, glinting gold beneath the lamplight. Her pretty hands held a book. Alas! not invitingly toward me, but open on her knees. Her eyes were bright with interest, but not in her father, she did not look up when I entered; she had not even heard my knock. Her body was there, but she herself had sailed away without me! She had embarked alone upon that great sea of the soul which receives all streams and washes all shores.

Alone I stood there, repeating sadly a word she could not hear; Good-bye, Goodbye little Beth! Good-bye. I'm glad you can read.

The children are Beth, Lawrence, Theodore, Margaret and cousin David. The photo is printed from a glass slide.

IN THE PREFACE OF *When Little Souls Awake*, he declares that everyone must get control of himself and that "the intellect, the heart and the will must be adjusted to the conditions of spiritual life."

In a chapter entitled, "His First Victory" he tells of the contest of wills brought about by a son's refusal to hang up his cap as he had always done in the past. With utmost patience HTB sits out the child's tantrums and refusal to act until finally the little boy rushes across the room and picks up his hat and puts it in the appropriate place and runs to his father's arms and says, "I love you."

HTB writes:
Could it be possible? After all those tears... It seemed to me then that I had heard in my own home the echo of that sublime faith, "Though he slay me, yet will I trust him."

In a chapter "His First Prayer," he writes of another son who with a friend took eggs from a hen's nest and broke them on a stone to see what was inside:

Do you know what would have happened to those eggs if you had left them alone under the hen?," the father asked. The son answered, "They'd have been chickens. There were fingers and big dark eyes all sound asleep in them when we opened them!"

In realization of what he had done, the son pressed himself into the hollow of my arm. Presently I heard a sob and a wet little face was thrust beneath my chin, out of a contrite heart came the broken words, "Oh papa, I'm so sorry I did it. I didn't know it would be so bad." The father asked, "Now are you going to tell God that you are sorry you took the lives of his little chickens?" At his mother's knee, after some prodding the son prayed, "Please forgive me for killing your little chickens when they were asleep. I won't never do it again if you will." When he rose from his knees a new look of happiness was in his face, and the joyous kiss he gave his mother was like a thanksgiving to God.

FAMILY TRADITIONS

Henry and Josephine saw to it that their children would remember traditions from their childhood.

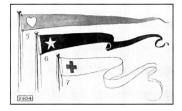

FLAGS

In *The Flush of Dawn*, Henry calls the flag, "that most abstract of symbols, that most familiar of geometric design.

HTB writes:

One summer's day at Siena when that beautiful medieval spectacle, Il Palio was in progress, I saw for the first time the splendid effects produced by symbolic flags. Then and there I determined to enrich the life of one home, at least, with fluttering pennants and rich banners, gracefully riding the free air, and every one significant. I made designs in color that night at Siena and sent them home in a letter and by New Year's some of the flags were finished.

The production began with astronomical pennants marking the changing of the seasons. Followed by Holiday banners, then House Flags—marking marriage, the birthday pennant and the Banner of Friendship. These flags were flown on the appropriate occasion, from the top of the Tower on Trustworth. There was a special chest for their keeping.

Camp Chickadee.

Son Theodore tells this story:
In those days, the flags flying from the Tower could be seen from the ships at sea. On one occasion, when Pa was known to be returning from Europe we decided to surprise him with a new flag. We made a banner in black with a skull and crossbones on it and flew it from the tower.

HTB writes:
The flag is a living thing, like an open fire; it claims attention, appeals to the imagination, beckons to the spirit; but it can adorn a day only for seeing eyes; it can restore the past only for those who remember, it can "make tomorrow a new morn" only for those who anticipate the moment when it shall be flung to the breeze.

CAMP CHICKADEE

HTB had a small camp built on Trustworth property. He named it "Camp Chickadee." Here there were many gatherings of family and friends for picnics and discussions of flowers and birds. The camp served as an educational get-away and a social meeting place.

HTB loved nature and was particularly drawn to early mornings. "Have you been up at four o'clock one of these superb May mornings? You ought to do that at least once a year, to see the majestic rising of the curtain of the night, and to hear the prelude to the day's message played to the full company of birds."

Also on the Trustworth property was another cottage—called "Bramblecroft." HTB always loved naming structures and particularly trees, giving them identification and appreciation.

ORIGINAL BOOKPLATES

HTB designed original bookplates for each of their children, always incorporating the particular child's interest.

ORIGINAL CHRISTMAS CARDS

Every Christmas Henry and Josephine would send out an original Christmas Card—designed by Henry with a photo or sketch or quotation and beautiful lettering. This tradition continues on through several members of subsequent generations.

LETTER WRITING

HTB wrote thousands of letters—often embellishing them with his own drawings. One of the recipients of his letters was a little girl named Gretta. She was the daughter of one of his friends in the Burrough's Club in Willoughby, Ohio. The letters were always in his beautiful script, accompanied by exquisite designs or little playful squirrels climbing around the top of a chimney.

I have been fortunate to meet Gretta who is now in her nineties and she has provided me with some of the notes HTB sent her when she was a little girl.

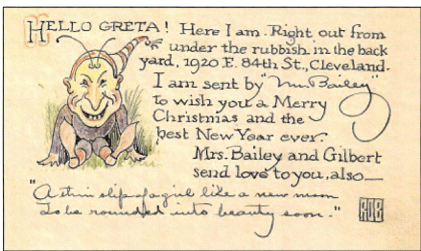

Daughter Margaret's description of her father:

Father was the same person at home that he was in public life. Relatively free from inner conflict, he had an uncomplicated character that was almost childlike in its simplicity. To be sure it was not always restful to live with such an enthusiastic and impulsive person, who shouted in his cold bath on winter mornings and in summer was up before dawn to traipse the woods looking for birds, or to paint a sunrise, write a chapter for a new book or compose a half dozen letters in his neat, rounded long-hand. He often worked about the house and yard, being a good carpenter and a good gardener. When exasperated by what he called "the innate perversity of inanimate objects," he would shout "Rats!" or (the strongest expletive I ever heard him use), "Baked rabbits on a half shell!" All his life he was demonstrative of his affection for Jo and we grew up in the security of their mutual love and trust. Mother was always there, providing our day-to-day care, discipline and training, and father was forever going off and coming back, yet, miraculously, he managed to be as much a part of our lives as she. He expected instant obedience, without argument, to whatever he or mother asked of us, but such direct orders were few. There were certain standards that we knew we had to meet. Of precepts, I remember best, mother's "Use your own judgment" and father's "Be different: the Lord doesn't want us to be like a row of potatoes." He taught us to swim and paddle a canoe, make a garden, handle tools, take photographs and develop them. He took us for long walks and picnics in the woods and marshes and taught us the names of the butterflies, birds, flowers mushrooms and stars. He provided a music teacher for us and listened to our progress with delight. He designed (and mother made) symbolic flags which we flew on birthdays, anniversaries and holidays to honor our many house guests. He read poetry to us, led us in family worship on Sunday mornings (praying with characteristic urgency), and went with us to church and Sunday School. All his wide-ranging reading and traveling liberalized but did not weaken his religious faith. His belief in God and his Christian commitment were always central to his life.

A man of strong convictions, he was "outspokenly intolerant of both alcohol and tobacco. He was not interested in organized sports. He never went hunting or fishing as taking wild life was repugnant to him. He was not an animal lover: he disliked dogs and barely tolerated cats (and then only in winter when they could not harm birds). He did, however, love children and young people. If, in his travels, he saw an unknown child, weary and bored, he would take his small scissors from his pocket and begin cutting out the delightful three-dimensional paper animals that were his own invention. The great sorrow of his life was that his youngest child, Gilbert, was born brain-damaged, and he spent even more time with him than he had with the rest of us.

Gilbert with his nephew, Jim Bailey circa 1930.

CHAPTER IV
GILBERT

"All my life has been a joy, rich in unexpected and delightful opportunities which have led me into every state of the Union, Canada, and the continents of the old world. During these years I have had my tribulations, of course, and one supreme sorrow."
—HTB in *Yankee Notions*

HENRY AND JOSEPHINE'S YOUNGEST CHILD, Gilbert, was born at home. Deprived of oxygen at birth, he suffered brain damage.

Both of his parents searched everywhere for the help that would provide the way to independence for their son, but at that time there were few special schools or institutions dedicated to the mentally handicapped, and they determined to take care of him at home and not institutionalize him or accept government support for his care. His mother's one wish was that she would outlive him, but this was not to be.

Both Josephine and Henry were devoted to Gilbert. He was a happy, outgoing child who radiated the love and care given him.

The care of Gilbert affected the whole family. Margaret, Gilbert's sister, writes:
Father spent even more time with him (Gilbert) than he had with the rest of us, taking him for walks, reading to him, working around the place with him, trying to find or create educational facilities at a time when only custodial care was available for the mentally handicapped. Father always believed, in spite of what the doctors told him, that some day my brother would be helped, but this was one thing that even his energy and optimism could never bring to pass.

Fall's Field
North Scituate
Henry Turner Bailey
1927

GILBERT ALWAYS LOOKED FORWARD to visits from members of his family and delighted in showing them around Trustworth. Often there was a jigsaw puzzle which he was in the process of putting together. This he could do very rapidly, and to everyone's amazement could even accomplish with the pieces upside down with the picture not visible!

When my husband and I and our two children were in Boston for a convention, we took a side trip to North Scituate to see Gilbert. Our children, Gretchen and Carl were young, elementary school age and had heard of Gilbert but had never met him. As usual Gilbert was all smiles and delighted to show us around. He took us up to the tower. No one had cleaned it, probably for years, and dust and flies covered the window sills. Gilbert, always happy to be boss, ordered our daughter Gretchen to blow the flies off the sills. Gretchen hated bugs of any kind and we all had a good laugh as she tried to blow the flies away.

Later when we were downstairs the caretakers told me that I had better rescue my husband, Bob. Gilbert had him down in the cellar, cleaning up. We could hear Gilbert saying "Bob, pick up that and put it in the barrel." Bob obliged, wanting to please him.

When the family moved to Cleveland for HTB to become Director of the Cleveland School of Art, Gilbert received the same loving care he had at Trustworth.

From the *Plain Dealer,* August 14, 1921:
Any pleasant Saturday afternoon or Sunday, winter or summer, a gray haired man of 56, accompanied by a boy of 14, may be seen trudging along some unfrequented road in Cleveland's outskirts. If you see them in the spring or summer, you may observe that they stop frequently to inspect some roadside wild flower at close range, or to pause on the brink of some tree-lined vista. The man is Henry Turner Bailey, Director of the Cleveland School of Art, and the boy is Gilbert Bailey, his son, out for a good time.

In an article written in 1928 about a garden in the heart of Cleveland, HTB writes:
My boy Gilbert and I have tramped the same trail through the Glen once a week, rain or shine, snow or blow, from October lst to May 31st, for three consecutive years. We have seen a total of ninety-seven varieties of birds in the heart of a modern industrial city of a million inhabitants. There is a rough bench we have built of driftwood in the most tangled thicket of the Glen. Seated there in the fading light of a winter afternoon, sheltered, cozy, in the lovely silence, busy noisy Cleveland seems a thousand miles away—and peace and joy enfold me like the warm soft arms of my Mother, when I was a tired little boy.

In a later newspaper article, HTB writes:
Our youngest son (Gilbert) is now of college age. With him I spend a half-day every week in the wild places about Cleveland. For two years we have kept a census of the birds found in Lakeview Cemetery, in the middle of the easterly metropolitan area. We know just when the redwings go in the fall, and just when the fox sparrows pass through on their way to Canada in the spring. We know that on the third Saturday in January falls the low tide of the year in bird life, and that a few song sparrows spend the winter by the brookside in a bog full of cattails.

IN 1930, HTB CONCLUDED his position as Director of the Cleveland School of Art (now the Cleveland Institute of Art) and returned to Trustworth. Josephine and Beth (Elisabeth) again took care of Gilbert in the familiar surroundings of Trustworth.

Reuinion in the 1950's: Lawrence, Elisabeth, Theodore, Margaret and Gilbert.

From a brief family history on the care of Gilbert by Paul Miles, son of Margaret Bailey Miles:

Because Josephine was strong in her opinion that Gilbert should never be a burden on society and that the family should do everything it could to care for him, her will stated: "So long as my son, Gilbert T. Bailey, shall live, the Trustee shall have the right to use the income and such portion, if any, of the principal as the trustee may deem necessary, and in such manner as the Trustee may deem best, for the care, comfort and support of my son, Gilbert T. Bailey and of the Trustee."

No Trustee has ever availed herself or himself of the right to use income and principal for his own benefit. Further, the Trustees have never taken estate funds in compensation for the many hours of time applied to their duties over many years. The family, including their children, grand-children and great grandchildren, have always agreed fully with Henry and Josephine's desire to use the estate resources for Gilbert's care. It is interesting to note that their other two sons, Lawrence and Theodore, while providing regular moral support and financial advice to the Trustees, also provided regular monthly donations to help cover costs for Gilbert's support until their deaths in 1974 and 1976 respectively.

When Josephine died in 1942, Elisabeth continued Gilbert's care at Trustworth until her death in 1955 and then Henry's sister, Sarah (Sally) followed and eventually caregivers were hired. When Margaret, Gilbert's sister, was widowed, she moved Gilbert from Trustworth to her house on Country Way and cared for him there. Before her death in 1988, she indicated that she did not want another generation to have this responsibility and suggested that Gilbert be placed in a home for special needs. "Gilbert was admitted to a nursing home in 1988 where the family continued to support him and he was cared for with skill and love" writes Paul Miles.

PAUL TOLD THE FOLLOWING STORY about Gilbert's stay at the home, and I recount it here as I remember it. The residents were told there would be a spelling bee and Gilbert asked if he could be a part of it. The Director said, "Well, Gilbert, can you spell bunny?" Gilbert thought for a minute and said, "R-A-B-B-I-T" to the amazement and amusement of the Director. Paul explained that HTB used to draw a bunny for Gilbert using the letters R-A-B-B-I-T with the two tall loops of the B's being the bunny's ears and obviously Gilbert never forgot!

In 1995 Gilbert died at age 90, having outlived his parents and all of his brothers and sisters. Josephine's desire to use all of the proceeds of the estate to care for Gilbert having been met, Trustworth was sold out of the family and HTB's study that had remained unchanged some sixty years after his death, now belonged to others. According to Josephine's will, the remaining assets were distributed equally to the grandchildren of Henry and Josephine.

The Trustees for Gilbert over the years were: Elisabeth Bailey, Margaret Bailey Miles, Paul B. Miles and Matthew B. Miles, co-Trustees.

Grandchildren at Trustworth.

CHAPTER V
HENRY AND JOSEPHINE'S
GRANDCHILDREN

HENRY AND JOSEPHINE had seven grandchildren. Lawrence and Gladys had a son—Robert (Bob); Margaret and Max had three children—Matthew, Paul and Josephine; Ted and Helen had three children—Jim, Jack and Jean.

GRANDCHILDREN AT TRUSTWORTH

The picture shown here was taken probably in the thirties and is of all but cousin Robert (Bob) who was not at Trustworth at the time. Gilbert is standing to the right. The cousins are pictured in a cart that was kept in the backyard. Matthew, Paul and Josephine lived in North Scituate and Jim, Jack and Jean were there from Cleveland. Their father, Ted had lost his job when the stock market crashed and the family spent one year living at Bramblecroft, a cottage on the grounds of Trustworth.

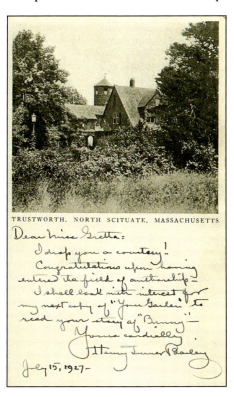

TRUSTWORTH, NORTH SCITUATE, MASSACHUSETTS

HTB's and Josephine's letters have many references to their grandchildren. Matt, Paul and Josephine lived in North Scituate and Henry and Josephine's letters indicate how much they loved them and how appreciative they were of having them near by.

Grandchildren, Jean and Jack at Chautauqua Institution.

GRANDCHILDREN AT CHAUTAUQUA

A second picture is of Jack and Jean. Our Mother sent it to Grandpa and Grandma Bailey and HTB sent a letter back saying how amused he was by the picture.

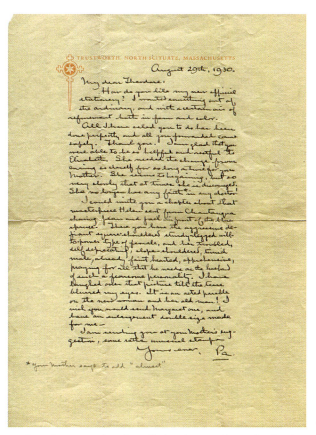

I have his original letter in his distinctive handwriting and have included here a printed copy:

I could write you a chapter about that masterpiece Helen sent from Chautauqua showing Jean and Jack in front of the blue spruce. There you have the aggressive defiant square-shouldered sturdy-legged will-to-power type of female, and her troubled, self-deprecating, slope-shouldered, timid male, already faint hearted, apprehensive, praying for all that he needs as the husband of such a fearsome personality. I have laughed over that picture till the tears blurred my eyes. It is an acted parable on the new woman and her old man! I wish you would send Margaret one and have an enlargement double size made for me. Yours ever, Pa

The TRAVEL CLUB

WILL celebrate Lincoln's birthday, February 12th
by traveling

TO EGYPT

Under the eloquent and graphic guidance *of*

HENRY TURNER BAILEY

Director of THE CLEVELAND SCHOOL *of* ART

WHO *has been chosen to conduct this expedition because he can be relied upon to avoid all that is more ancient than 8000 B. C., in the land of the Pharoahs, concentrating, rather, upon such modern art and living beauty as are exemplified in temples, tombs and pyramids, the glories of Egyptian sunsets and the graceful gambols of camels and hippopotami by the waters of the fabled Nile.*

IT *is peculiarly appropriate that the birthday of* ABRAHAM LINCOLN *should be thus celebrated because Abraham discovered Egypt (see Genesis XII.) and Lincoln freed the Africans who had been in slavery in Egypt long before that discovery, and are so pictured upon Egyptian monuments If these two historic events had not taken place there would be nobody to celebrate in the* MARTIN AUDITORIUM *of the Y. M. C. A., at 8:15 P. M., February 12th.*

CHAPTER VI
CHOOSING LIFE'S WORK:
TEACHER AND TRAVELER

"You wanted to go on with your catching of butterflies, and your breeding of ducks; you wanted to show what your father's farm could produce; you wanted to live selfishly and die rich, right where you were born. You have never thought to ask your master about that. He has shown you to yourself tonight."
—HTB from *Victorious Surrender*

ALTOUGH WRITTEN USING ANOTHER NAME, Hubert, this story is obviously autobiographical. After a speech Henry gave at graduation the realization that people were listening, for the first time he felt "the delicious sting of power over the minds of his fellow men."

Thus began an artist's life of teaching, lecturing and travel.

Henry's position as State Supervisor of Drawing for the State of Massachusetts took him over the state into every town and village. His transportation was mainly by train and provided much time for reading. His education was continued through his reading of Shakespeare, Thoreau, William James, Swedenborg, St. Augustine, Voltaire, Plato, Walt Whitman and his favorite, Emerson.

A newspaper article headlined: "Supervisor Bailey Grew Burnsides for Dignity":
Mutton chops are getting rarer every day. That is the kind Dean Henry Turner Bailey is wearing in his 1902 picture. It wasn't a question of mustaches with him, for mutton chops were his defensive camouflage. "That was when I was 21 years old and supervisor of art in the Massachusetts schools. When the children saw me coming they used to say, 'Oh teacher, here's a boy to see you.' so I had to grow burnsides to help me out of the difficulty," said Dean Bailey.

Margaret writes:
In later years his children were touched by his deference for their college

degrees, knowing that in the humanities, his education was better than theirs.

In addition to local trips, Henry broadened his education through extensive traveling throughout the world. "In 1898 he was appointed United States representative to the International Art Congress and took the opportunity to spend eight months studying French in Paris and traveling about Europe. But when at last he came home to Trustworth and Josephine and the children, he vowed he would never again be away so long—and he never was." However, he led travel parties to Europe in 1903, 1904, 1907, 1908, 1912, 1920, 1924 and 1928. Margaret, having accompanied him on one such trip wrote, "I know he was a stimulating party leader, inspiring others by his immense enthusiasm for scenery, history, art and architecture. How could one ever forget his moving appreciation of St. Francis when we visited Assisi?

If he found out that any member of his party was insulting to hotel employees, or condescending to shop-keepers, or critical of food, or boasting of how much better the plumbing was in America, he did not hesitate to call the whole group together for a scathing lecture on travel manners.

ON HIS TRAVELS, HTB produced numerous pencil sketches that demonstrated his superb draftsmanship and his love of architecture and nature.

Cleveland newspaper, writer unknown:
More daring and as interesting as his pencil drawings are his pocket sketches from "over there." There are forty tiny watercolors, each a part of the story of his travels... Everyone of his pocket sketches carries with it his impressions, a quotation that explains, or a bit of whimsy. Who but Henry Turner Bailey would ignore the conventional view of the Acropolis and paint the back door of that famous pile of rock.

HTB, THE ARTIST

DEAN BAILEY'S ART was simply a part of everything he did. His oil paintings capture the sunrises that he loved. Their coloring is subdued, warm and textured. His expertise in sketching is evident in all of the drawings he did of his trips and the architecture and nature surrounding North Scituate. His drawings were primarily pencil sketches, sometimes with a watercolor wash. He was admired for his blackboard drawings with chalk that were spontaneous and used to further the points of his lectures. An artist he was but teaching was primary to his life.

A sketch of St. Peter's in Rome while traveling through Europe.

When asked questions about his painting, HTB said, "I shall never be a great painter. I am too old for that. And I paint only that I may remain sensitive to color. You get color in the sunrise. What do I do with my paintings? Oh, I've exhibited some of them, sold a few and swapped a lot of them for things I value more."

THE SCHOOL ARTS MAGAZINE

In 1903, HTB left his employment with the state to start a monthly magazine to help public school teachers of art. For the next fourteen years he edited *The School Arts Magazine*. He also added a publication for children, *Something To Do*.

Margaret Bailey Miles writes:
Only one who has experienced it can appreciate the immense amount of labor entailed in such editorial work, not to mention the business end of it, for which he had no aptitude. The magazine failed as a business venture and it took him years to pay the debts incurred, but it is still in existence today.

ALTHOUGH HE SOMETIMES FELT "the call to preach," HTB's unique ability to relate to people through lecturing and teaching led to his appointment as Director of the Chautauqua Art School and then Dean of the Cleveland School of Art.

The Bourzi of Nauplia, 1924.

VOLUME XII   SEPTEMBER, 1912   NUMBER 1

THE SCHOOL ARTS MAGAZINE

HENRY TURNER BAILEY, Editor

THE SCHOOL ARTS PUBLISHING COMPANY

BOSTON, MASSACHUSETTS

TWENTY-FIVE CENTS A COPY   TWO DOLLARS A YEAR

HTB on the historic walk at Chautauqua, circa 1915.

CHAPTER VII
CHAUTAUQUA AND THE ARTS &
CRAFTS QUADRANGLE

"A stranger coming to Chautauqua is struck with the general cleanliness of the place, with the good sense exhibited in cutting and pruning and protecting the trees, with the lack of advertising signs, the adequate new fence with its dignified gates, temperately ornamented."
—HTB in a 1906 issue of the *Chautauquan Daily*

CHAUTAUQUA INSTITUTION WAS FOUNDED in 1874 as a Methodist summer camp for school teachers. It is located in western New York State on Chautauqua Lake and is the original of many summer educational camps that have taken on the Chautauqua name. It is still vibrant today. The nine-week season brings thousands from around the country to take part in an outstanding combination of arts, education, religion and recreation.

From an undated pamphlet, author anonymous:
A man who has made his mark deeply on Chautauqua is Mr. Henry Turner Bailey of the Arts and Crafts School. He could not only teach, but could lecture on art or history in a most fascinating manner, all the time drawing pictures on the blackboard with both hands at once. Under his care the Arts and Crafts shops were assembled, grew into a village, and later found their home in a series of fine buildings on College Hill.

WHEN HTB FIRST CAME to Chautauqua as Director of the Art School in 1906, the Arts and Crafts School was housed in a collection of small wooden, clapboard stick-style buildings near the road gate at Ames and Palestine.

Avron Posner, in a history published May 9, 2000, writes that "HTB was committed to Arts and Crafts Education and in 1909 with the construction of the Arts and Crafts Quadrangle."

From Av Posner's *"The Arts and Crafts Quadrangle, Henry Turner Bailey, The Arts and Crafts Movement at Chautauqua, New York":*
Architect Kelsey suggested a complex at the North end of the grounds—Swiss German chalet in feeling. This concept was not built. In its place, HTB developed plans with Franklin J. Kidd, of the Buffalo-based architectural firm of Green & Wicks (designers of the Albright Art Gallery, Albright-Knox). Together these men laid down the lines of the Plan—Vincent, Bestor, Green, Wick, Kidd and Bailey.

The new school was conceived as a large open quadrangle with a covered walkway extending around the inner circumference—begun with a central pavilion "Two Chimneys" for lectures.

This portion of the building is also known as "Two Stack Hall" and has been named for Henry Turner Bailey by his descendants and bears a plaque. There are two flanking wings in the shingle style with bright airy studios.

Posner says:
The columns that abut the walkway and surround the quadrangle reflect a simplified classicism—they are 'milk bottles' with minimal capitals and without bases. Construction was by George W. Rowland and the initial block was finished for the summer of 1909 with the second section begun in 1910. The entire project was finished in 1917 when Chautauqua boasted that no other summer school in the country...has so complete and picturesque a plant.

Posner says of HTB, "He felt that Chautauqua should be a place where Beauty is studied, created, and reflected in the physical facilities."

THE QUADRANGLE IS STILL in use today with young artists praising its concept as open and conducive to collaboration and inspiring to the creativity of the artists working there. The northeast side of the quadrangle is open and the land in that direction remains as originally conceived, a beautiful vista of grass and trees leading all the way down to the lake.

The Arts and Crafts Quadrangle at Chautauqua Institution.

HTB LECTURES AT CHAUTAUQUA

HENRY TURNER BAILEY was a frequent lecturer at Chautauqua—often on the Amphitheater stage, as well as at the Arts and Crafts Quadrangle in Two Stack Hall where his lectures attracted standing room only crowds. His first year at Chautauqua (1906) he is quoted often in the Daily immediately beginning to put the imprint of his philosophy on his new surroundings.

From the Chautauqua Archives and their invaluable collection of *Chautauquan Dailys* comes the following record of Henry Turner Bailey's words:
A more beautiful Chautauqua can only come through the sinking of personal whim and pride beneath catholic, teachable, cooperative spirit.

HTB ENCOURAGED THE PLANTING of native plants and good signage in plain roman with shading and a great stone tower containing a chime of tuned bells, and a clock that gives the correct time and one deep-toned bell for announcements in the center of the Plaza.

A similar tower was built, but it is on the lake adjacent to Miller Park.

In 1909, HTB gave a series of lectures in the Amphitheater on "Beauty in Common Things." He used his blackboard illustration approach. A reporter for the *Daily* wrote, "his blackboard drawings are made with astonishing rapidity."

Timothy Hatherly
"Merchant Adventurer"
In his fifth century.

1927

HTB stated:
People are under an obligation to learn to recognize beauty and then take their part in making the world more beautiful. In order to have beauty the elements are: consistency, variety and orderly arrangement. Things are beautiful which represent fine proportion, rhythmic measure, and harmonious sequences of color.

HTB's observations on decor:
The prim monotony of the old fashioned parlor made it unfitted for anything save funerals and weddings.

Most rich men's houses are ugly because large numbers of Americans have an idea that if the heterogeneous mass of architectural elements they assemble in a house is expensive enough, it is therefore beautiful.

The reason people are so anxious to change wallpaper and other decorations so much is that they were never right to begin with.

HE URGED HIS AUDIENCE members to "begin by looking at the humble things around us—then the trees—learn to see pictures everywhere."

In 1916, HTB gave a lecture series in the Amphitheater on "The Enjoyment of Beauty in Nature" which drew very large audiences. He said, "There are three perennial hungers: Knowledge, love, beauty. He said, "that there are some present who have seen nothing of nature."

He quoted Emerson in this regard:
> Alas thine is bankruptcy
> Blessed nature to see
> The brook sings on but sings in vain
> Wanting the echo in thy brain.

HTB writes:
We are not responsible for the faces we wear when we come into this world, but we are responsible for those when we go out.

HTB HAD A HABIT of naming trees which he said develop character with age. He mentions that he has "a branch of wild azalea which I have in my study at home. It is more beautiful now for I will not allow it to be dusted and a spider has woven a beautiful obligato about it."

HTB on trees:

Every tree has a different air and manner according to the place in which it grows just as the man raised in the country has a different manner from the one raised in the city.

Josephine Miles Schuman writes about some of the trees HTB named:

Lazarus, which he raised with block and tackle when it went over in a storm; Aunt Polly Peak's tree, where Deacon Peak used to go to pray for support when Aunt Polly was too much to bear; Jotham Wade, a cedar still beautiful, named for our ancestor; Demosthenes, 'The noblest white pine in Northern Ohio'; Job, the patriarch; Timothy Hatherly with a gate leading through the woods to Aunt Emma's house.

From *Chautauqua Daily* article on HTB lecture:

A number of complaints came to him about the care of trees at Chautauqua. With Mr. Bestor (then President of Chautauqua) sitting on the platform, Mr. Bailey said that he would not mention these things to Mr. Bestor in public but would have a private talk with him about them. Mr. Bailey said it was his wish that a sign worded as one over the piano in the saloon in a mining town in the west could be placed over Mr. Bestor's head. It read: "Don't Shoot the performer. He is doing the best he can."

From his diaries: July 26, 1911. Archives, University of Oregon
Supper at Bestor's cottage: Bestor, Bailey, Vincent, Hutcheson, and others.
"One of the jolliest occasions ever at Chautauqua."

In 1916 he gave a lecture on the Arts and Crafts Movement and from the Daily review:
"Mr. Bailey was heard by one of the largest audiences of the season and held them to the last word."

Expressing his philosophy, HTB said the following:
There is no doubt that we have a Renaissance in America, and that we are on the threshold of the greatest development of arts and crafts that the world has ever seen. He said that 1876 was followed by the most ugly art that the world has ever known. In 1893 at the World's Columbia Exhibition the beauty of the arts and crafts was astonishing. He encouraged the production of industrial objects that had beauty. While there is a limit to the material value, the spiritual or aesthetic may be increased in so far as the craftsman is skilled in transforming material to a thing of beauty. The promise of a beautiful life will be realized not for the few—the powerful and the rich as heretofore—but for the many.

IN 1916, DEAN BAILEY left his position at Chautauqua Institution to begin his tenure as Director of the Cleveland School of Art (now the Cleveland Institute of Art).

Henry Turner Bailey's affiliation with Chautauqua has continued through his descendants who still own property on the Chautauqua grounds. His great-great-grandchildren come back each year to enjoy the summer there.

HTB whipping up mushroom recipes for guests and family.

CHAPTER VIII
THE CLEVELAND SCHOOL OF ART -
"THE CHEERFUL DEAN"

"You have in Cleveland one of the most vigorous, one of the most hopeful art schools in the country." —HTB as quoted in the *Plain Dealer* two years before he became Director of the Cleveland School of Art.

IN A BOOKLET ENTITLED, *Cleveland Institute of Art (originally the Cleveland School of Art): The First 100 Years*, a chapter is devoted to Henry Turner Bailey's tenure as Director. The chapter is titled "Strengthening the Base." The dates of his tenure were from 1917 to 1930.

The report begins, "When gregarious and energetic Henry Turner Bailey joined the Cleveland School of Art in 1917, he was recognized at fifty-one as one of the nation's foremost men in art education."

"To his colleagues in the art community he was known as 'The Cheerful Dean'."

He rapidly became a booster of Cleveland as evidenced by this statement from him in 1919:
Cleveland just now is arriving at self-consciousness. Our parks and boulevards, the art museum, the new museum of natural history, the interest of industry in art, all presage great things in the artistic life of the city. No other city in the United States can compare with Cleveland in its interest in art; no other city in the world is so good to live in.

THE CLEVELAND INSTITUTE OF ART'S 100th anniversary publication speaks of HTB's devotion to religion, nature and art, and his distinguished reputation as a lecturer on art appreciation and his authorship of some twenty volumes. "For ten years he served as advisor to the education department of the new Museum of Art, also as director of the old Chamber of Commerce, President of the Cleveland Society of Artists and belonged to the Rowfant Club and the Writers Club. He was widely known for the all-day bird walks which he organized and which attracted nature lovers from throughout the area. He was one of the organizers of the Huntington Polytechnic Institute and served as its director.

From the *Cleveland Institute of Art's 100th anniversary:*
He was an artist and was particularly adept at pencil sketches and paintings. One of the activities that he is most remembered for was his leadership of one of the largest men's Sunday School Classes at the Baptist Church of the Master."

Dean Bailey's position at the CIA (Cleveland Institute of Art) began the same year that the United States entered into World War I, and his administration with faculty and students planned and carried out projects in support of the war—from posters to making of garments. In 1918, a course was established that taught 130 women to be occupational therapists with the goal of teaching arts and crafts to wounded veterans still in the hospitals. This course was offered in conjunction with the Red Cross and Western Reserve University.

Early Cleveland School of Art building on Magnolia Drive in University Circle.

AT THIS TIME there was a new interest in the application of art in industry and Dean Bailey believed that good design did not have to be expensive. He wanted to see good artistic design in every day objects and promoted the same. "He felt there were three components to improving industrial products: training in technique, training in taste and training in design."

Dean Bailey is quoted in the Anniversary Book as saying:
Knowing the best that has been produced, the craftsman with the skilled hand and the illuminated mind will be able to lead in the production of objects acceptable to a person of taste, objects worthy of a place in the ever-lengthening history of the arts, objects that cultivated people will be glad to buy. The best trade in the world goes to the nation that produces the finest things.

THE CLEVELAND MUSEUM OF ART

HTB worked with the Cleveland Museum of Art and was a frequent lecturer there. Both the Cleveland School of Art and the Cleveland Museum of Art worked together to relate their institutions to the community and instigated programs to meet the community's needs.

Early in Dean Bailey's directorship, the May show was established. It soon became one of the nation's largest and best known annual juried exhibitions of work by artists and craftsmen from one region. In the first two years, 1919 and 1920, the May Show was organized by the Cleveland Art Association under the direction of Mrs. Frank W. Wardwell and the Art Museum Director, F. Allen Whiting.

By 1924, eighty-four of the 150 artists and craftsmen whose work was accepted had Art School connections, providing a showcase for their work. During Dean Bailey's tenure, the Art School library was expanded and in the 1920's there was a waiting list for students to enter the Art School. Plans were begun to build a new school for art instruction, architecture and industrial arts in cooperation with Western Reserve University.

A newspaper article of the time stated:
Our eminent fellow-townsman, Henry Turner Bailey, Dean of the Cleveland School of Art isn't saying much these days, modestly suggesting that his plans for a greater art center in Cleveland are merely tentative. But that is sufficient. Anyone who has met the Dean who knows his intense love for the finer aspects of life, his willingness to work and to sacrifice for the

attainment of ideals, can take for granted that if Dean Bailey has set his heart upon $5,000,000 worth of new buildings for the local School of Art, he will get them.

THE PLAN FOR THE new building was called the "Vision Plan" and Bailey pointed out that it would "provide the three sources of reference material that a art school needs within easy reach: a natural history museum for the study of beauty in nature, a historical museum for original documents as to men and events necessary to the designer and illustrator and an art museum to furnish cultural background and standards of taste."

The depression delayed the construction of the new building for several decades. It now occupies the corner of East Boulevard and Bellflower, the site that was chosen for the construction in the twenties. In the year 2012, The Cleveland Institute of Art is making a move and further expansion of its facilities in the previously renovated Ford Plant (now the McCullough Building) further east on Euclid Avenue.

The tenure of HTB at the Cleveland School of Art was characterized by the emergence of what became known as "The Cleveland School," and it included such artists as Paul Travis, Frank Wilcox, Henry G. Keller, Victor Schreckengost, Charles Burchfield, Edris Eckhardt and others (see below). Even today special exhibits are arranged showcasing these artists.

Additional "Cleveland School" Artists:
Kay Dorn Cass, Thelma and Edward Winter, John Paul Miller, Rolf Stoll, Peter Paul Dubanowicz, Kenneth Bates, Carl Gaertner, Frederick A Miller, William and Leza McVay and Julian Stanzak.

I. T. Frary of the Cleveland Museum of Art summed up HTB's contributions as follows:
Henry Turner Bailey has placed the study of art and various technical subjects within the reach of young people who otherwise would have been denied such opportunities; as a platform lecturer speaking with equal authority on painting, sculpture, architecture, costume, handicraft and the every day things of life, he has thrilled countless audiences with a clearer understanding and appreciation for the things that make life finer and better. His writings and lectures are punctuated with scintillating humor, often illustrated by clever sketches. Few speakers possess in a higher degree the gift of holding an audience and conveying to it his own enthusiasm and optimism.

THE ANNIVERSARY PAMPHLET recalls that "In 1930, prompted by his wife's declining health, Dean Bailey submitted his resignation to go back to their home in North Scituate, Massachusetts, and he wanted to do more lecturing and writing. The trustees accepted his resignation with regret."

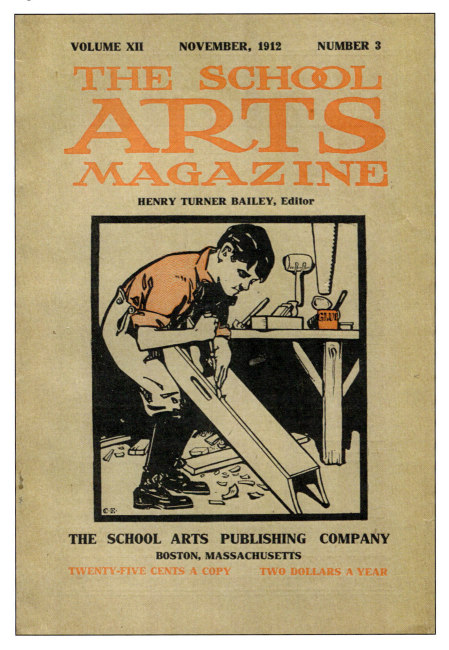

THE BEAUTY LOVER'S
✢ ✢ CREED ✢ ✢

✢ I believe in Beauty as the manifestation of triumphant life.

✢ I believe in looking for Beauty everywhere; watching for it, searching for it in the great and in the small, in the unusual and in the commonplace things of this wonderful world. ✢

✢ I believe in working for Beauty always; planning for it, trying for it in the making of all that has to be made, and in the doing of all that has to be done. ✢

✢ I believe in living the Beauty-ful life; a life in right relation to the lives of others and in harmony with the eternally unfolding life of God.

✢ ✢ ✢

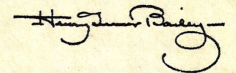

CHAPTER IX
LECTURES AND OPINIONS

"Happy as he was when tramping in the woods, painting or traveling. I think he was happiest on the lecture platform."
—Margaret Bailey Miles

HTB WAS RENOWNED for his lectures and in his record year, he lectured four hundred times.

Margaret writes:
From his earliest lectures at a summer school on the island of Martha's Vineyard in the nineties, to those he gave after his retirement ('Because now' he told me with a twinkle, 'I have to scratch all over the hen yard for a living.') he was at his best as a public speaker. The volumes and volumes of lecture notes that he left, carefully filed according to the towns in which they were given, in every state in the union, attest to his thoughtful preparation. Even his humorous anecdotes were not carelessly thrown in; each one was there to illustrate a point in a memorable way. He never wrote out what he had to say, but spoke from his notes so informally that it seemed spontaneous. Most of his lectures were on art and art appreciation, but others were on education or religion, and he was in demand as a commencement speaker, guaranteed not to bore a young audience.

From the *Nashville Banner,* February 10, 1915:
Henry Turner Bailey, the distinguished editor and lecturer who will spend Friday of this week in Nashville, is perhaps better known and more generally beloved by teachers in all parts of the country than any one person engaged in the education and uplift of the youth of the country... It is because Mr. Bailey loves people that he so instantaneously appeals to all classes of auditors. The simplest and the most erudite sit at his feet, learning things new, for he seems to know thoroughly something others have never thought of.

One charming story HTB told:
Once upon a time, in the state of Massachusetts, there was a little boy who didn't want to do anything but draw. The little boy's mother was greatly worried about her son and went to the state supervisor of drawing and said, "I don't know what to do with my son. He has just finished grammar school but he doesn't want to go to school any more; he doesn't care to do anything but draw." "Then let him draw," the state supervisor said, "See that he finishes high school, but keep him drawing. Buy him books about drawing, and see that he has every opportunity to develop his talent."

THAT LITTLE BOY GREW UP to be the famous illustrator, N. C. Wyeth. The state supervisor was Henry Turner Bailey. HTB told this story to introduce N. C. Wyeth at a luncheon given for the artist at the Hotel Statler, Saturday, December 9, 1922 when Wyeth was in Cleveland as the guest of the Halle Bros. Book Shop.

An article in the *Cleveland News*, in 1923 entitled, "And Now The City's Done In Vivid Orange," reads as follows:
It was an overwhelming outburst of hideous orange paint that obscured the perfection of the May day with the clouds of a war between the economists and the esthetes. The issue was—orange paint on safety zone markers, city automobiles, on parking signs, park benches, refreshment stands and the Public Square benches.

Mayor Kohler said the clubhouse at Highland park golf links if it needs paint, will get it—orange paint! So will all other paintable outdoor city possessions, he said.

However, Henry Turner Bailey, Dean of the Cleveland School of Art spoke his mind, scoring heavily. "Things of different functions and different sizes should be different in color. A conspicuous color that is perfectly appropriate for safety zone designation is not the right thing for seats in the parks. By the same token, the bigger an object is the less color it should have… Seats in the park should be of some restful color."

Purchasing agent, Burt Atkinson, made no secret of the fact that a "very low price had been secured by buying a large quantity of the same color." Cleveland, fifth city of the land once known as the "Forest City" and recorded in many a stirring chapter of political history as "The City on the Hill" has been rechristened. And Kohler's cohorts, full-panoplied in spotted jumpers and armed with brush and paint pail go marching on.

MY FATHER, TED BAILEY, filled an album with clippings about his father's lectures. These clippings reveal HTB's multitude of interests and often expressions of strong opinions. He commented on clothing, nature, architecture, government, photography and a myriad of other subjects.

HTB on Architecture:

Giving words to his interest in architecture, HTB commented on the new Euclid Avenue Temple and was quoted in the *Plain Dealer* of March 1924:
It would be difficult to name in the entire city of Cleveland a more consistent design, both in form and in color, than this handsome structure. It rests on a lot with perfect dignity and eternal calm. This temple in its appearance is the embodiment of the very spirit of the race. Solid, of enduring material, venerable looking, richly colored, bright eyed, imperturbable, calm. It sits in its place on busy, noisy, restless Euclid Avenue, like Simeon of old in Jerusalem, 'waiting for the consolation of Israel.'

When I was in the Temple Tifereth Israel in the 1990's, I was surprised to hear my grandfather quoted by the Rabbi. In a dedication piece, HTB calls the New Temple, "The mountain of the height of Israel."

HTB's description of the Temple follows:
Like a mountain top its dome first catches the rays of the rising sun; bears aloft through the winter its crown of snow; receives with perfect grace the drifting shadows of the clouds at noonday; transforms itself into a great jewel of amethyst against the golden west at sunset and becomes a heap of silver beneath the magic of the moon.

As a building it is one of the masterpieces of the city. Of an ancient style adapted to modern needs, pleasing in mass and charming in detail, rightly placed in its peculiar lot and tastefully planted, it is a perpetual object lesson to all in architectural beauty.

From a lecture in 1925:
No future history of architecture ever will be written without some mention of the Woolworth Building in New York City. It is a magnificent structure, with all the care for details that makes all the best cathedrals in Europe such wonderful structures.

HTB HELD STRONG OPINIONS and was not reluctant to express them.

On Apartments:

HTB's strong opinions sometimes reflected the more Victorian thinking of the times:
The apartment house is one of the greatest menaces to civilization. My reasons for calling it a menace are these: No room for children ... loss of education children gain through cooperation in home chores, and of nature study out where there are grass and trees and sunshine ... Idleness among women, therefore, discontent leading to questionable pleasures which open doors to immorality.

On Charles Burchfield:

It is good to note that he showed more flexibility in other areas. Although his own paintings and sketches were very traditional, he was an admirer of one of his students, Charles Burchfield, whose paintings challenged the current style of painting.

Of Burchfield's work, HTB wrote the following:

Mr. Burchfield sees nature with keen penetration. To him nothing is commonplace, everything is radiant with beauty all its own. His pictures shock the observer into looking at nature from a new angle. Burchfield paints not merely what he sees, but in addition what he feels about what he sees. His pictures reflect states of mind induced by experiences with the outside world. His pictures reflect moods. They must be judged by those who feel rather than those who carry a Kodak.

On Museums:

In some regards HTB was ahead of his time as is evident in this quotation from one of his lectures about museums. An article in a newspaper carried this title, "Municipal Nickel-in-the-Slot Art" lectures were advocated by Henry Turner Bailey, prominent art authority.

HTB said:

I would like to see installed in the Boston Museum of Fine Arts a slot machine where, upon the dropping of a coin, by phonographic reproduction, I could get an explanation of the particular subject I wanted to understand and appreciate.

SOUNDS LIKE THE FORERUNNER of today's technology that enables visitors to art museums to access information on individual objects of art.

From the *Christian Science Monitor,* January 16, 1915:
Mr. Bailey deplores what he terms the present-day tendency to use museums as storage houses for valuable objects and places for conservative gatherings. He would reform art museum administration so that the working man could drop into the building on his way home and find something that would interest him immediately and without effort.

On Dress:
We cannot give attention to the finer qualities of dress without becoming a little finer ourselves.

IN RESPONSE TO A QUESTION about good taste in dress, Dean Bailey said, "Brilliance of color should be used for the small places; and dull colors are better suited to the large figure as they are applied in art for background spaces." He has been quoted as saying, "God didn't clothe the elephant the way he did the hummingbird."

One lecture, urging women to age gracefully as do trees, brought forth the following response in a local paper from "Styles in Song" by Styletta.

Response to Lecture on Beauty:
> Our Dean Henry Turner Bailey
> Says that women hourly, daily
> As they older grow, should be
> Unaffected as a tree:
> They should never camouflage,
> But be proud to show their age;
> So the Art School chief asserts;
> He is right - but how it hurts!
> I would ask him, "Is it square
> For Dame Nature, Queen of Mothers,
> To make some of us fair
> Yet deny her charms to others?
> Ah, Dean Bailey, we but try
> Her mistakes to rectify;
> All of us would like to please
> Manly eyes, as do all trees!

On Religion:

There can be no warfare between a true religion and a true science. The house of Truth is not divided against itself, nor does it need at the present time such buttressing and bracing with straws as these nervous 'Fundamentalists' are offering us.

From his diaries, June 28, 1908, Greece - Archives, University of Oregon:
Went to the Russian church where we heard some good music. Went to the English Church for service at 11:00. As usual rather stupid and uninteresting.

From a chapter in *Yankee Notions,* about his "Victorious Surrender":
When a man in these days begins to talk about his 'religious experience,' heads nod upward while an eye is winked and mental question marks appear within the minds of bored and old fashioned twaddle. And yet, deep in the heart of every man there is a suspicion that there is in the universe Something his mother thought of as God, and with Which or Whom some sort of a personal relation seems possible, to some people, which gives joy and strength and peace.

The moment we begin to think seriously about it, we find we are living in two worlds. One is the physical world, where we have to eat and sleep and work to earn a living and dodge automobiles to keep alive. But every normal human being lives in another world, a world that the spirit of man has created through the centuries.

On Leisure Time:

Leisure is at once the most precious and the most dangerous gift to mankind. But leisure is the most dangerous of gifts in the hands of those who do not know how to use it wisely.... Character is determined partly by what a man does for a living; but more largely by what he does with his leisure time.

On Composition in Painting:

At a Roundtable in 1923:
The first step in making a picture is to woo and win a single idea. The second step is to wean the idea from its relations and the third step is to see to it that there goes into that picture only legitimate offspring of that idea.

On Cemeteries:

Article in Cleveland, "Topics", January 8, 1927.

When asked about improving the design and layout in cemeteries, HTB responded:
Memorials in cemeteries have troubled me for a long time. Upon investigation, I found that the cost of much of the ugliness and inappropriateness in these memorials is due to the interplay of four factors:

1. Eager and tasteless agents.
2. Tenderhearted and anxious mourners.
3. Over zealous dealers in stoneware.
4. Ignorant, untrained and tasteless designers.

I am not so sure but there is a fifth reason, i.e. the man higher up, who wants to pocket all of the profits, instead of sharing them with well-trained architects and sculptors.

On Outdoor Parlors:

The back yard is the best room in the house. The cure for too much of the world is more of the earth. It is a good thing to take down the front fences, but I want a back yard where I can do as I please.

On Beauty of the Home:

Begin with what you have. See how few things you can get along with, and have them as beautiful as you can afford.

American houses too frequently are over furnished.

On Education:

There are no more important studies in the school curriculum than drawing, nature study, poetry and music.

On Goals:

Men fail only at what they aim at. They had better aim at something high.

On Business Men:

O tired business man, O selfish egoist, O anxious father, the cure for too much of the world is more of the earth; for too much of self, more of others; for too much introspection, more of the spontaneous self-expression your children will teach you, if you only give them half a chance.

On Life:

HTB from *The Magic Realm of the Arts:*
As I look back over my own life, I can recall the names of hundreds of people, good, bad and indifferent; but the names that shine in my sky at night, as stars forever, are the names of those who revealed to me the gates of pearl: My mother, whose feet knew every golden square of the pavement beneath the arch of the gate called Poetry; Ellen Gannett, who invited me to enter the shining portal of Religion; Derithe Hoyht, who led me through the gateway to the Painters; William Atwood, who revealed to me the green pastures and still water beyond the gate called Nature Study; Ned Baldwin, who opened for me the gate of Music; Dr. William T. Harris, who turned my feet into the pathway to the gate of Philosophy. Are there not such stars in your sky?

And when I cease to cast a shadow upon the green earth that I have loved so long, and become just a memory to those who have known me— my children and grandchildren, my pupils in the public schools, in the night schools, in the art school, I would be content if any of them were to say of me, "Whether he was a sinner, I know not; one thing I know, he opened my eyes to see one of the gates of pearl."

CHAPTER X
COMMUNITY INVOLVEMENT

SCITUATE HISTORICAL SOCIETY

In 1917, the Society celebrated its one-year anniversary and the speaker was HTB.

I quote from the minutes of that event:
Henry Turner Bailey, who is widely known as an art critic and lecturer, presided at the exercises in the auditorium of the church. Silas Pierce, president of Drake played the organ voluntary, and the Rev. Lawrence Perry made the opening prayer. One of the most interesting parts of the program was the singing of the old hymn "Duke Street" in the fashion of the Pilgrims. Frederick P. Bailey acted as verger and "ruled off" the hymn a line at a time, the audience singing each line after him. Franklin P. Barnes accompanied the singing on a bass viol made in Scituate in 1836 by Shadrach and Asa Merritt. Miss Agnes Bachelder Edwards sang "Long, Long Ago" and other old songs, accompanied by Miss Minne L. Harrington.

Mr. Bailey, the presiding officer, was the principal speaker. In his address he pointed out that the organization of the society was due to the efforts of Harvey Hunter Pratt. He suggested that a book, *Scituate's Own* should be made up from the poems of Woodworth, Bliss Carman, Richard Hovey and Edward Wesley Cushman—the Thoreau of Scituate, who is in a serious condition as the result of an accident.

Following the address a quartet which included Miss Elisabeth Bailey, Miss Esther M. Spaulding, Waldo Bates, Jr., the Rev. J. West Thompson sang "The Old Oaken Bucket."

The program closed with a benediction by the Rev. J. West Thompson and the singing of "America."

THE FIRST BAPTIST CHURCH OF NORTH SCITUATE

Sally Bailey Brown writes of the Memorial windows:

The stained glass windows in the auditorium were installed in 1901. These were designed by Deacon Henry Turner Bailey with the symbols and beatitudes chosen with great care, each representing the life and character of the people whose names were inscribed below:

> Abiel Cudworth and Joanna
> Deacon George W. Bailey and Hannah Briggs
> James and Selina Briggs
> Deacon Charles Bailey and Eudora
> Deacon Freeman Gannet and Miss Ellen
> Ellen B. Vinal and George Vinal
> Jotham Wade Bailey and Helen Seaverns Bailey
> Henry Austin Seaverns and Mercy Litchfiled
> Joseph Tilden Bailey

CLEVELAND

HTB involved himself deeply in the Cleveland Community serving on many Boards including Torch, the Cleveland Chamber of Commerce, the Huntington Foundation and others. Several organizations in particular occupied his time.

TORCH

From a newspaper article of a presentation to Torch members:

The most popularly brilliant address of the week was made by Henry Turner Bailey, of Cleveland on 'Leisure.' The audience was in humor for his scintillations. Mr. Bailey's personality is peculiarly fascinating. He has the grace and ease of conversation with no trace of oratory, no gestures, no dependence on play of voice or features, just rippling, jingling phrasing of unexpected interpretation of every day life.

THE HENRY TURNER BAILEY'S MEN'S CLASS

The Baptist Church of the Master:
Over one hundred men gathered regularly to hear Henry Turner Bailey discuss religion, nature and life in general. At the first annual banquet of the Men's Class, the invitation stated: "Here is a chance to hear Dean Bailey deliver one of his famous Chalk Talks. This is an event you will remember."

AT THE SECOND ANNUAL BANQUET, the invitation stated, "The class is growing, 123 men were out last Sunday. The Standing Room Only sign was hung up before the Dean started his talk."

An announcement was made that Dean Bailey would be giving a series of lectures on "Art in the Service of Religion" to the Men's Bible Class at the Church of the Master at East 97th street and Euclid Avenue.

The announcement read:
He plans to show why there was no art during the first century; how symbolic art was the next inevitable step; why art was forced to play a large part during the years of the falling Roman Empire; why it became standardized; how in Italy it revised and put forth fresh growths; trace the causes of its brilliant flavoring in the thirteenth century; and then follow the gradual transitions from the childlike story-telling art of the renaissance to the art of the nineteenth century influenced by archeology, to the art of the twentieth reflecting modern psychology and religious idealism of the present time.

THE CLASS WAS OFTEN written up in the newspapers and HTB initiated Nature Walks through the Men's Club, leading to the formation of the Burroughs Club in Willoughby.

THE BURROUGHS CLUB OF WILLOUGHBY

HTB advises:
Search out his wondrous works not with a gun but with a field glass and a camera.

Mission of the Burroughs Club:
The Burroughs Club is dedicated to the preservation and conservation of the wild bird and wild flower life in this section, and yearly brings to Willoughby noted speakers and visitors interested in these objectives.

Captain George Finally Simmons in *Outdoor Adventuring in Northern Ohio:*
The Burroughs Nature Club of Willoughby, Ohio is known as one of the most active in America. And, though many of the members watch first for birds when rambling through the woods and across the fields, a surprising knowledge of flowers and trees has developed throughout the  Willoughby section. Nothing could be more lovely than Cushman's Ravine, where I wandered with Dean Henry Turner Bailey of the Cleveland School of Art.

Annual Field Day, Burroughs Hike from the *Willoughby Republican,* **May 23, 1924:**
Each year in May the Burroughs Nature Club has a sort of 'Day of Days' set apart for a high pressure hike covering as much territory as possible with the objective of a long list of birds and wild flowers. The Burroughs party held at the new Andrews Hall Saturday night is said by many who where in attendance to have been one of the most delightful affairs that has been held in Willoughby in a long time. One hundred and thirty-six guests were served an excellent supper served by the Andrews girls.

It would be difficult for any writer to express in cold type the sparkle, charm and human interest of Dean Bailey's talk. It was one of the most inspirational that has been heard here at any time.

From the *Willoughby Republican,* **June 1, 1923:**
Henry Turner Bailey does not believe in losing the best part of the day when he goes hiking or marsh exploring. That was the reason why, probably, that when he notified some Willoughby friends that he would go out Decoration Day, he told them to be ready at 5:00 a.m. and brought breakfast along.

M. Shipman and Frank Shankland were the Willoughby folks, other friends of Bailey's from Cleveland making up the party. They breakfasted at 7 at Mentor marsh. There was a pot of Boston baked beans which the men buried in the fire a la Massachusetts picnic style. There were sliced cucumbers, with a special dressing prepared by Mrs. Bailey. The picnic breakfast eaten, the party explored until 10:30 and then returned to Willoughby. Mr. Bailey brought along all the food even having a knife and fork and spoon for each member of the party and butter with ice on it.

From the *Lake County News Herald,* April 17, 1926:
"Visitors May be Nature Lovers and Prominent But Cop Gets Them When They Speed." Visitors may be nature lovers and exponents of the beautiful in art, but the traffic cops at Mentor-on-the-Lake are no respecters of persons, it appears, when it comes to speeders. According to reports, Henry Turner Bailey, Dean of the Cleveland School of Art; C.M.Finfrock, Dean of Western Reserve University Law School; F.N. Shankland of the Andrews Institute for Girls; Professor Hulme of Natural History and Raymond T. Kelley of the Metal Alloys Co., were hastening to get in or from Mentor marshes Saturday afternoon when Constable Cobb halted them in the name of the law.

Tis claimed that Mr. Kelley was the lead driver and that the others of the party were endeavoring to keep up with him. At any rate, all of the drivers were to appear before Mayor Taylor at Mentor-on-the-Lake Tuesday night, and what direful sentence was meted out has not been reported.

THE BURROUGHS CLUB 80 YEARS LATER

An invitation to the 80th annual May Hike in 2001 recounts the founding: "In May of 1921, Dean Henry Turner Bailey of the Cleveland School of Art called Frank Shankland and C.M. Shipman in Willoughby, proposing to bring some 'bird sharps' out to Willoughby for a day of tramping. Now 80 years later, we continue this annual custom, though we no longer begin the day with 6:30 a.m. breakfast cooked at Gully Brook."

From Carl T. Robertson in the *Plain Dealer:*
So many years ago I cannot with certainty fix the date, I became a member of the group which under the guidance of Dean Bailey and of Messrs. Shipman and Shankland of Willoughby each May in the midst of warbler season crawled out of bed before daylight and assembled before daylight for the annual May walk. Ever the leader was Dean Bailey; the leader and the inspiration.

IT HAS BEEN THIS writer's privilege to meet the daughter of C. M. Shipman, Gretta Pollister of Willoughby. Gretta and her husband are now in their nineties and have provided me with memorabilia including letters written to her by HTB—complete with his original pencil sketches.

CHAPTER XI
JOSEPHINE AND THE RETURN TO
TRUSTWORTH

*"All his life he was demonstrative of his affection for Jo and
we grew up in the security of their mutual love and trust."*
—Margaret Bailey Miles

HENRY AND JOSEPHINE'S LOVE was lifelong though Josephine's
health was a concern throughout. She suffered from pernicious anemia
and took medication for it all of her life.

When Henry retired from the Cleveland Institute of Art in 1930 at
the age of 65, the family returned to North Scituate and Trustworth and
looked forward to resuming the life they loved in the countryside of their
youth.

Elisabeth took care of the move from Cleveland. Back at Trustworth,
she and Henry took care of Josephine who by now was bedridden.

Henry wrote to son Ted's wife Helen, August 1930:
Mother Bailey, while slowly improving, is unable as yet to write letters.
She wants me to thank you for your lovely letters to her, and to assure you
that she loves you always as a very dear daughter. She says that Jimmie
is right, that things are getting worse and worse so far as enjoying me and
others are concerned, and that she would love to tip up his face, look into
his brown eyes and give him loving kisses. She sends more to happy faced
Jack and to sweet Jean.

In a subsequent letter, HTB writes:
Mother Bailey's recovery is sure, the doctors say, but very, very slow.
She sits up daily, is able to eat three meals a day, and would be about the
house were it not for her head. Her nervous trouble is bad, and keeps her
in bed most of the time. Elisabeth and I are camped on the job of getting
her well.

Just one year later in August of 1931, Henry wrote the following to his Cleveland friend, Raymond Kelley after her doctor came up with a new treatment:

To see her now you would think she had never had a sick day in her life. She has regained her normal weight, and acquired the right amount of good red blood. She is out of bed by ten o'clock in the forenoon, and about the house at work as of old. She has to be careful not to overdo and not to receive more than one or two visitors at a time. She is now able to read and to be read to, and to write a letter or two every day. After taking her meals for seven months alone in her chamber, with no desire for food—merely as prescribed medicine, she is now at table with us twice a day, and is beginning to enjoy life again... Margaret and her three dear little children are a great delight to her. The boys think Grandpa's house such a delight that they make mention of it in their prayers!" Ever cordially yours, Henry Turner Bailey

NOW WITH JOSEPHINE'S HEALTH improving, the family looked ahead with optimism and anticipation of sharing the happy days to come.

Margaret wrote:
Father's spirits rebounded, and I remember, one of those summer mornings, of hearing his laughter ring out when I was a hundred yards from the house.

HENRY WAS SCHEDULED to give a lecture in Chicago in November with the plan to come home for Thanksgiving. While hurrying in the rain to avoid a car turning into the street he was crossing, he slipped and fell on the wet car tracks and broke his kneecap. Taken to the hospital he was cared for and son Ted was called with the message of the accident and that his father was doing well.

Henry writing of the accident to his friend Raymond Kelley:
It was the most instantaneous, surprising and unnecessary event of my life. And of course, it comes at a bad time for Mrs. Bailey. She is still far from well, although the anemia is under control, they say, and her blood count back to normal.

After nine days, HTB was operated on and he wrote to his friend:
My split tendons and my broken knee cap were properly adjusted and laced into shape with Kangaroo tendons from Australia. The day after, I felt like a stewed mushroom not fit to eat. They tell me that the operation was successful and that I am doing well. I know nothing but what I read in the papers.

The Spire
N⁰ Scituate, Mass
Sept. 10. 1919

THEN TED RECEIVED a second call saying that unexpectedly his father had died. The doctors thought a circulating blood clot from his injury had reached his lungs and stopped his breathing. Ted was devastated. My brother, Jim, remembers Dad turning from the phone and saying, "Pa is dead. I will never be truly happy again." Now the son made the hard trip to Chicago to bring back his father's body by train to Massachusetts and to his grieving family.

At the conclusion of the memorial service with Henry's body on view, Josephine could not let go of him and her children told her, "That's not Pa. Pa is gone. That's just his body." Then Josephine said, "I loved that too."

Following the burial Josephine wrote the following to Henry's dear friend in Cleveland, Raymond Kelley:
I want you to know that your friendship for Mr. Bailey gave him much happiness. I cannot write as I would like about him, what he was to me and how empty life is without him. For over sixty years we were lovers —and companions—and I find myself with my daily life ever turning to him for assurance and guidance. He always said when we talked of the future—'We will go on together' and added 'May you have a peaceful Indian summer to your life which you richly deserve.' Gilbert is broken hearted.

And again to Mr. Kelly:
My sons and daughters are so splendid and try hard to make me comfortable. Max and Margaret are near us and help us daily. The dear children are wonderful. The days are so lonely and the nights are worse. Everyone said the spring would bring me help, but my lover is not here and how can June be June without him.

> And so, how sad the lovely landscape's face;
> How wan the mellow moonlights' silver grace!
> Better for me the autumn chill and sere
> Than June, since you who loved it are not here.

I am striving daily to do as he would wish me to do. My children need me and want me.

Sincerely yours, Josephine Bailey, Mrs. Henry Turner Bailey— This name I shall never give up.

Upon her father's death, Margaret quoted Robert Louis Stevenson:
"The noise of the mallet and chisel is scarcely quenched, the trumpets are hardly done blowing when, trailing with him clouds of glory, this happy-starred, full-blooded spirit shoots into the spiritual land."

HENRY'S FRIEND, RAYMOND KELLEY preserved in an album the words of Edgar A. Guest from his poem, "To a Kindly Scholar." I quote here the last verse:

> Oh, gentle friend who is no more
> Would you had left behind
> For us to use whose need is sore
> The riches of your mind.
> And yet we know, who shed a tear
> Beside your flower-strewn grave,
> How very much while you were here
> And willingly you gave.

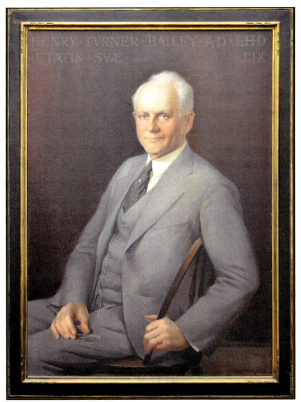

Portrait by Ralph Stoll

CHAPTER XII
TRIBUTES

SCITUATE

From the *Scituate Newspaper:*
A tall pine fell in the sudden death of Henry Turner Bailey. With a tremendous energy, Mr. Bailey vitalized every path which his footsteps trod.

CHAUTAUQUA

Rebecca Richmond in her 1943 book, *Chautauqua, An American Place*, wrote perhaps the warmest and most moving remembrance of Henry Turner Bailey's tenure at Chautauqua:

The man whose name and personality gave form and fame to the Arts and Crafts Movement at Chautauqua, and provided one of the liveliest chapters in its school history, was Henry Turner Bailey. He was editor of the well-known School Arts Magazine. He wrote and he spoke with authority on "How to Look at Pictures;" No one could surpass him in his particular province, say those who heard him, for he was a tireless student of the history of art, an enthusiastic teacher and an artist himself.

He brought a philosopher's approach to his work: art he said would lead to a lifelong interest in almost anything. He had a fine, strong, simple religious faith, entirely without cant, and believed as profoundly as did Bishop Vincent that living and learning should be one. With all this, he was of an active temperament, and when he joined the Chautauqua staff in 1907 and became head of the Arts and Crafts, his first plans were for more permanent and beautiful housing for the Village workshops. The cloistered quadrangle that now overlooks the Lake from the north end of the grounds was built under his direction. Students in handicraft and in art have filled its unpretentious studios and classrooms in varying numbers ever since. Mr. Bailey's own administration lasted until 1916 when he became obliged to give all of his time to his duties as Dean of the Cleveland School of Art (now the Cleveland Institute of Art). It is no reflection on his co-workers or successors to say that the importance of the arts and crafts classes began to decline when they lacked his guiding genius. The teachers who came after him were gifted and enthusiastic. But no one was available who had so vivid a conviction of what Art should mean to all of life, combined with the ability to share his vision with the student who expected to make some form of art a career, or the student who sought merely to train her hands for her own satisfaction. To this day the cloisters retain a serene charm for all who enter them. Those who knew Mr. Bailey at Chautauqua say warmly, "He did a great deal for us." One infers that the character of the man and his aspirations spread an influence about them that Chautauqua has retained ever since.

CLEVELAND

From Cleveland Newspapers:
The best book that Henry Turner Bailey wrote was never printed and cannot be. It is the book that he lived.

Perhaps no Clevelander ever had a wider circle of sincere personal friends than Henry Turner Bailey. And this is probably the highest tribute that can be paid to the memory of any man.

It was Dean Bailey, more that any other individual, who brought to Cleveland an awareness of art. Now he is gone.

A teacher he always was, until finally a whole region looked to him for guidance.

He was one of the greatest interpreters of beauty who had ever been among us. He did wonders in opening the eyes and the minds of Clevelanders to the beauties in nature and art which they had passed by unrecognized. He was a creator of cultural appreciation who has left his impress permanently upon us. —Cleveland Mayor Burton

Dean Bailey was great because he saw the universe with a comprehending eye, loved the universe, and communicated that love to those around him with enthusiasm and vigor. —David Dietz in the *Cleveland Press*

But Dean Bailey, tho remembered for what he did, will be remembered more for the way that he did it. —*Cleveland Press*, Nov. 27, 1931

From the Burroughs Club:
"A good friend and a good man is gone. No man was better known and better loved and more generally admired in Cleveland than Henry Turner Bailey. No man ever lived who was a more ardent enthusiast in the pursuit both of the beautiful in nature and of the enchanting facts of nature lore. And no companion of the sylvan shade was ever more sympathetic with every strange or lovely thing God has made."

He taught us all to see the beauties in the commonplace and things all about us. —Frank Shankland, Burroughs Club of Willoughby

Sunday Mens' Group:
Dean Bailey was one of the richest men I have ever known. His attitude to life was wholesome, wise, courageous and hopeful. He was at home with the form, line and color of art composition. His rapid sketches of trees, fruit and flowers seemed almost by magic. It was a delight to see him, with one swing of the arm, draw a perfect circle on his blackboard.

With him nature at her best was gracious, beautiful and bountiful. How much he knew about the birds! How eagerly he listened to their songs and watched their every movement. In the open fields and leafy forests, he had a boyish abandon. A sense of humor was a vital part of his many-sided character.

To Dean Bailey came deep sorrow, frustrations and crosses but with it all life was good, to be lived courageously, abundantly, gladly to the end. With him the good life, the religious life, was not so much to be proclaimed as to be lived. —Harris R. Cooley, Member of HTB's Sunday Men's Club

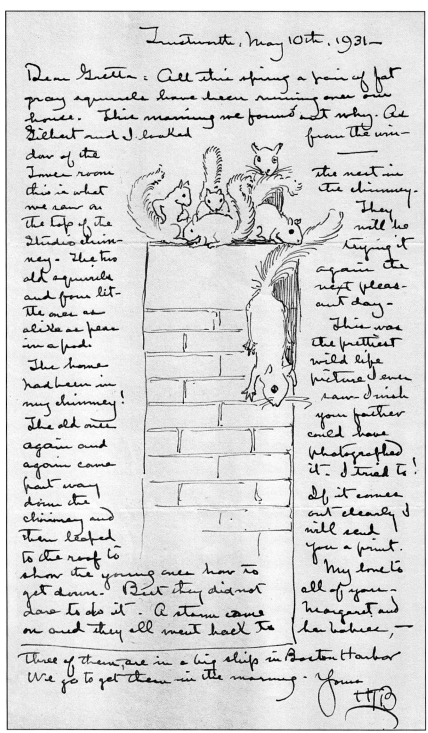

Innisfail, May 10th, 1931—

Dear Gretta: All this spring a pair of fat gray squirrels have been running over our house. This morning we found out why. As Gilbert and I looked from the win-dow of the Tower room this is what we saw on the top of the Studio chim-ney. The two old squirrels and four lit-tle ones as alike as peas in a pod. The home had been in my chimney! The old ones again and again came part way down the chimney and then leaped to the roof to show the young ones how to get down. But they did not dare to do it. A storm came on and they all went back to the nest in the chimney. They will be trying it again the next pleas-ant day. This was the prettiest wild life picture I ever saw — I wish your father could have photographed it. I tried to! If it comes out clearly I will send you a print. My love to all of you — Margaret and her babies, —

Three of them are in a big ship in Boston Harbor We go to get them in the morning. Yours

Delightful sketch sent to Gretta, daughter of HTB's good friend in the Burrough's Club.

APPENDIX

TIMELINE IN THE LIFE OF HENRY TURNER BAILEY

Henry: Born 1865 - Died 1931
Josephine: Born 1865 - Died 1942
Engagement to Josephine: 1882
Marriage and completion of Trustworth: 1889

CHILDREN

Elisabeth   Born 1890 - Died 1955

Lawrence   Born 1892 - Died 1974

Theodore   Born 1894 - Died 1976

Margaret   Born 1899 - Died 1988

Gilbert   Born 1905 - Died 1995

LIFE'S WORK

Director of Drawing - State of Massachusetts: 1887 to 1904
Founder of the School Arts Magazine: 1903
Director of the Art School at Chautauqua, New York: 1906-1916
Director of the Cleveland School of Art: 1917-1930
(Now the Cleveland Institute of Art)
Travels and lectures throughout his professional life

RETIREMENT: Return to Trustworth: 1930

RESOURCES

Chautauqua Archives: *Chautauquan Daily*

Cleveland Institute of Art: First 100 Years 1882-1982, by Nancy Coe Wixom

Chautauqua, An American Place, by Rebecca Richmond

Henry Turner Bailey and the Arts & Crafts Quadrangle, by Av Posner

Scituate Historical Society: Minutes

University of Oregon: Archives Diaries and Sketches

MAGAZINE ARTICLES OF INTEREST
Colonial Homes: February 1993
Classic Interpretations: Article and photos of Henry Turner Bailey's Home, Trustworth
Old House Interiors: Fall 1996, Trustworth: The Educator's Office

FAMILY AND FRIEND RESOURCES
Margaret Bailey Miles - Memories of HTB
Sarah Bailey Brown - Essays
Elisabeth Tova Bailey - Poem
Paul Miles - Article on Gilbert & photos & prints of material from University of Oregon
Josephine Miles Schuman - Information on Trees
Raymond Kelley - Clippings and Letters
Lawrence Bailey - Genealogy
Theodore Bailey - Clippings and correspondence
Cleveland Plain Dealer
Cleveland Press
Cleveland News
Henry Turner Bailey - his many books
Gretta Pollister - Photos & Letters & sketches

BOOKS AND PAMPHLETS
BY HENRY TURNER BAILEY

A Partial listing:
Yankee Notions
Pleasure from Pictures
Photography and Fine Art
Twelve Great Paintings
The Magic Realm of the Arts
Art Education
The Victorious Surrender
Symbolism for Artists
Famous Painting Books
Madonnas, Landscapes, Pastorals, Children, & Interiors
The Tree Folk
Nature Drawing
When Little Souls Awake
To You
Instruction in the Fine and Manual Arts in USA
Booklet Making
Art in the Schools
The Art Museum as a factor in Industrial Development
The History and Ideals of American Art
The Flush of Dawn
The Blackboard
The City in Refuge
The Blackboard In Sunday School
Arts & Crafts in the Public Schools
Booklet Making, An Art-Craft Problem
Founder and Editor of the School Arts Magazine
How to Arrange Flowers
All For You

Note: Some of these books are available on the internet.

GENEALOGY

LINE NUMBER ONE: Henry Turner Bailey's line

William Brewster (Mayflower)	married	Mary (Mayflower)
Mary Brewster 1645	married	John Turner
Lydia Turner 1675	married	John James
John James 1700	married	Eunice Stetson
Eunice James 1729	married	Charles Turner
Rev. Charles Turner 1756	married	Mary Rand
Charles Turner 1789	married	Hannah Jacobs
William Turner 1829	married	Sarah Tilden
Eudora Turner 1864	married	Charles Edward Bailey
Henry Turner Bailey 1889	married	Josephine M.Litchfield

Children: Elisabeth, Lawrence, Theodore, Margaret and Gilbert

LINE NUMBER TWO: Josephine Litchfiled's line

Degory Priest (Mayflower)

Mary Priest	married	Phineas Pratt
Aaron Pratt 1735	married	Sarah Pratt
Jonathan Pratt 1730	married	Hannah Whitcomb
Hannah Pratt 1760	married	James Litchfield
Joab Litchfield	married	Hannah Willcutt
Abraham Litchfield 1823	married	Rachel Nichols
Israel Litchfield	married	Rebecca Litchfield
Josephine Litchfield 1889	married	Henry Turner Bailey

Children: Elisabeth, Lawrence, Theodore, Margaret and Gilbert

PHOTOS AND ILLUSTRATIONS

PHOTOGRAPHS
Eudora, Henry's mother
Eudora at 90
Young Henry and Josephine
Trustworth
Henry and Josphine's children
Children going to school
Camp Chickadee
Gilbert and Jim
Brothers' and sisters' reunion
Grandchildren at Trustworth
Grandchildren at Chautauqua
HTB at Chautauqua, 1915
Arts & Crafts Quadrangle
Arts & Crafts Quadrangle plaque
HTB picnic
HTB cooking
Cleveland School of Art Building
HTB at work
HTB with friend and camera
Memorial stained glass windows
Henry and Josephine
Josephine & Henry Christmas card
HTB portrait, Ralph Stoll

ILLUSTRATIONS
Ravenna sketch, 1924
Letter to Gretta
Sketch of mice
Bookplate
Christmas card
Postcard to Gretta
Sketch of Falls Field
Travel Club Poster
Sketch of St. Peter's
Pencil sketch of Europe trip
School of Arts Magazine
Tree sketch, Timothy Hatherly
Beauty Lover's Creed
The Spire
Letter to Gretta with squirrels
Sketch of St. Paul's

LETTERS
Ted and Helen Bailey and Henry
and Josephine correspondence
Raymond Kelley and Henry and
Josephine correspondence

RESOURCES
Sarah Bailey Brown's Essays
Margaret Bailey Miles - *Memories of HTB*, *Cleveland Institute of Art Anniversary Book*
Cleveland Museum of Art
Chautauqua Archives:- *Chautauquan Daily*
Paul Miles - History of Gilbert
HTB Books: *Yankee Notions*, *The Flush of Dawn*, *Magic Realm of the Arts*
University of Oregon: Diaries and Sketches provided by Paul Miles
Av Posner - *The Arts & Crafts Quadrangle*
Josephine Miles Schuman - Trees
Gretta Pollister - Photos, letters and drawings
Elisabeth Tova Bailey - Poem